First World War
and Army of Occupation
War Diary
France, Belgium and Germany

46 DIVISION
Divisional Troops
Divisional Trench Mortar Batteries
17 March 1916 - 30 January 1919

WO95/2675/2

The Naval & Military Press Ltd
www.nmarchive.com
Published in association with The National Archives

Published by

The Naval & Military Press Ltd

Unit 10 Ridgewood Industrial Park,

Uckfield, East Sussex,

TN22 5QE England

Tel: +44 (0) 1825 749494

www.naval-military-press.com

www.nmarchive.com

This diary has been reprinted in facsimile from the original. Any imperfections are inevitably reproduced and the quality may fall short of modern type and cartographic standards.

© **Crown Copyright**
Images reproduced by permission of The National Archives, London, England, 2015.

Contents

Document type	Place/Title	Date From	Date To
Heading	WO95/2675/2 Divisional Trench Mortar Batteries		
Heading	Mortar Btys.		
Heading	War Diary 46th: Divisional Artillery Medium Trench Mortar Batteries March 1st To 31st 1916		
War Diary	In The Field	17/03/1916	31/03/1916
Heading	War Diary. Medium Trench Mortar Batteries-46th: Divisional Artillery April 1st: to 30th: 1916		
War Diary	In The Field	01/04/1916	30/04/1916
Miscellaneous	Trench Mortar 46th Divisional Artillery Scheme of Training.	23/04/1916	23/04/1916
Heading	War Diary Medium Trench Mortar Batteries. May 1st: to 31st: 1916		
War Diary	In The Field	01/05/1916	31/05/1916
Heading	War Diary. Headquarters 46th. Medium Trench Mortar Batteries. June 1st: to June 30th: 1916		
War Diary	In The Field	01/06/1916	30/06/1916
Miscellaneous	U Day Wire Cutting.		
Miscellaneous	V Day Wire Cutting.		
Miscellaneous	W Day Wire Cutting.		
Miscellaneous	X Day. Wire Cutting.		
Miscellaneous	Y Day Wire Cutting.		
Miscellaneous	Time Table		
Miscellaneous	Time Table Y II Day.		
Heading	War Diary. 46th. Trench Mortar Batteries. July 1st: to July 31st: 1916. Vol 5		
War Diary	In The Field	01/07/1916	31/07/1916
Miscellaneous	Z Day. Bombardment.		
Heading	War Diary. 46th: Divisional Artillery Trench Mortar Batteries. August 1st: to August 31st: 1916. Vol 6		
War Diary	In The Field	01/08/1916	31/08/1916
Heading	War Diary. Trench Mortar Batteries. 46 Div Arty. September 1st: to September 30th: 1916. Vol 7		
War Diary	In The Field	01/09/1916	30/09/1916
Heading	War Diary. Heavy And Medium Trench Mortar Batteries. October 1st: to October 31st: 1916. Vol 8		
War Diary	In The Field	01/10/1916	31/10/1916
Heading	War Diary 46th. Divisional Artillery Trench Mortars November 1916. Vol 9		
War Diary	Bavincourt	01/11/1916	30/11/1916
Heading	War Diary. Trench Mortar Batteries. December 1st: to December 31st: 1916. Vol 10		
War Diary	Bavincourt.	01/12/1916	10/12/1916
War Diary	Henu	19/12/1916	31/12/1916
Miscellaneous	46th: Divisional Artillery. Trench Mortar Batteries. Training Scheme.	04/12/1916	04/12/1916
Heading	War Diary Trench Mortar Batteries. January 1st: to January 31st: 1917. Vol XI		
War Diary	Henu	01/01/1917	31/01/1917
Heading	War Diary Trench Mortar Batteries February 1st: to February 28th: 1917. Vol 12		

War Diary	Henu	01/02/1917	28/02/1917
Heading	War Diary. Trench Mortar Batteries. March 1st: to March 31st: 1917. Vol 13		
War Diary	Henu	01/03/1917	26/03/1917
War Diary	Henu	13/03/1917	31/03/1917
War Diary		01/03/1917	31/03/1917
Heading	War Diary. Trench Mortar Batteries. April 1st: to April 30th: 1917. Vol 14		
War Diary	L'anvin	01/04/1917	01/04/1917
War Diary	Mazingham.	02/04/1917	12/04/1917
War Diary	Mazingham	06/04/1917	09/04/1917
War Diary	L' Ecleme	13/04/1917	22/04/1917
War Diary	Bully Grenay	23/04/1917	30/04/1917
War Diary	Bully Grenay	26/04/1917	30/04/1917
Heading	War Diary. Trench Mortar Batteries. May 1st: to May 31st: 1917. Vol 15		
War Diary	Bully Grenay.	01/05/1917	31/05/1917
Heading	War Diary. Trench Mortar Batteries. June 1st: to June 30th: 1917. Vol 16		
War Diary	Bully Grenay	01/06/1917	30/06/1917
Heading	War Diary. Trench Mortar Batteries. July 1st: to July 31st: 1917. Vol 17		
War Diary	Sains-En-Gohelle.	01/07/1917	08/07/1917
War Diary	Boyeffles	09/07/1917	31/07/1917
Heading	War Diary. Trench Mortar Batteries. August 1st: to August 31st: 1917. Vol 18		
War Diary	Boyeffles	01/08/1917	27/08/1917
War Diary	Bethune	27/08/1917	31/08/1917
Heading	War Diary. 46th: Trench Mortar Batteries. September 1st: to September 30th: 1917. Vol 19		
War Diary	Bethune	01/09/1917	02/09/1917
War Diary	Sailly Labourse	03/09/1917	30/09/1917
Heading	War Diary. Trench Mortar Batteries. October 1st: to October 31st: 1917. Vol 20		
War Diary	Sailly Labourse	01/10/1917	31/10/1917
Heading	War Diary. Trench Mortar Batteries. November 1st: to November 30th: 1917. Vol 21		
War Diary	Sailly Labourse	01/11/1917	30/11/1917
Heading	46th. Divisional Artillery. War Diary December-1917. 46th. Divisional Trench Mortar Batteries.		
War Diary	Sailly Labourse	01/12/1917	31/12/1917
Heading	War Diary. Trench Mortar Batteries. January 1st: to January 31st: 1918. Vol 23		
War Diary	Sailly Labourse	01/01/1918	26/01/1918
War Diary	Gornehem	27/01/1918	28/01/1918
Heading	War Diary. Trench Mortar Batteries. February 1st: to February 28th: 1918		
War Diary	Gornehem	01/02/1918	12/02/1918
War Diary	Verchin	12/02/1918	26/02/1918
War Diary	Allangne	27/02/1918	28/02/1918
Heading	War Diary. Trench Mortar Batteries. March 1st: to March 31st: 1918		
War Diary	Verchin	01/03/1918	05/03/1918
War Diary	Fouguires	06/03/1918	07/03/1918
War Diary	Annequin	08/03/1918	28/03/1918
War Diary	Les Brebis	29/03/1918	31/03/1918

Heading	46th Divisional Artillery. 46th Divisional Trench Mortars April 1918		
War Diary	Field	02/04/1918	30/04/1918
Heading	War Diary. Trench Mortar Batteries. May 1st: to May 31st: 1918		
War Diary	In The Field	01/05/1918	31/05/1918
Heading	War Diary. Trench Mortar Batteries. June 1st: 1918 to June 30th: 1918		
War Diary	In The Field	01/06/1918	31/07/1918
Heading	War Diary 46th. Divisional Trench Mortar Batteries. August 1st: to 31st: 1918		
War Diary	In The Field	01/08/1918	26/09/1918
War Diary	No. 8206341 Cpl Key. Died Of Wounds.	27/09/1918	30/09/1918
Heading	War Diary. Trench Mortar Batteries. October 1st: to October 31st: 1918		
War Diary	In The Field	01/10/1918	31/12/1918
War Diary	Landrecies.	18/01/1919	30/01/1919

WO95/2675/2
Divisional Trench Mortar Batteries

MORTAR BTYS.

CONFIDENTIAL

WAR DIARY.

46th: DIVISIONAL ARTILLERY MEDIUM TRENCH MORTAR BATTERIES

March 1st: to 31st: 1916.

WAR DIARY or INTELLIGENCE SUMMARY

Army Form C. 2118.

Place	Date	Hour	Summary of Events and Information	Remarks and references to Appendices
	1916 March		In the 46th Division there are three Medium Trench Mortar Batteries, each with a personnel of 8 officers & other ranks. Nomenclature of the batteries is X46, Y46, and Z46 Medium Trench Mortar Batteries. The personnel of the batteries was trained at the Third Army Trench Mortar School and isolation almost amounting in the case of Y46 and Z46 batteries from the 4th Divisional Artillery. The personnel of Z46 battery consists of men drawn from the R.G.A., the two officers belonging to the R.G.A. Artillery. The officers attached to the three batteries are :— X46 battery. 2nd Lt. C. J. Davies from 3rd London Bty. R.F.A. Lt. F. J. Atkin from R.15e/g & 17 2nd Lon R.F.A. Y46 battery. 2nd Lt. S. Andertin(?) from 1st Midland Bde. R.F.A. 2nd Lt. A. Pepper from 2nd Midland Bde. R.F.A. Z46 battery. 2nd Lt. R. Sinclair from 146th Div. Amm. Col. 2nd Lt. S. Holmes from 2nd Midland Bde. R.F.A. The three batteries at present with the Division have each four 2" Trench Mortars. These mortars fire a projectile consisting of a bomb weighing 50 lbs, together with a tail weighing 10 lbs. The max. Ammunition range is 600 yards and the minimum 100 yards.	

Army Form C. 2118.

WAR DIARY
or
INTELLIGENCE SUMMARY.
(Erase heading not required.)

Instructions regarding War Diaries and Intelligence Summaries are contained in F. S. Regs., Part II. and the Staff Manual respectively. Title pages will be prepared in manuscript.

Place	Date	Hour	Summary of Events and Information	Remarks and references to Appendices
Battlefield	March 17th		Captain N.C. Brown gone to supervise the medium trench Mortar Batteries X146 Batty. moved from VILLERS CHATEL to ÉCOIVRES, and was attached to 150th Divl Arty. A.S.A. Ammunition Column. Y146 and Z146 Sgnd. wagon lines are at CAMBLAIN L'ABBÉ, and were attached to the Ammn. Column of the 2nd and 3rd Wilts. Bdes. respectively. 3 sections X146 Batty. were located to the 13th Infantry Brigade Y146 acting for the 15th and Z146 Batty. for the 14th. Moles and conditions were bad, a Battery is in the trenches and has to go at a time, plenty for firing Peace every so long. Two guns per battery are kept in action and reserve positions, and another gun is kept in the trenches to improve our own country.	Ap. 1
	18th		A position was selected for X146 Battery, which was to up the dig at night.	Ap. 1
	19th		A position was reconnoitred for Z146 Bty, X146 Bty. now in position.	Ap. 1
	20th		Z146 Bty. went into action.	Ap. 1
	21st		Aquiror along.	Ap. 1
	22nd		Y146 Bty. went into action in the evening.	Ap. 1
	23rd		A gun of our Y X146 Bty. registered.	Ap. 1
	24th		On Z146 Bty. front a mine was exploded by the enemy at night. Spectacle fort expld. as gun came in a bursts of sings by night did not appear to be fire.	Ap. 1

Army Form C. 2118.

WAR DIARY
or
INTELLIGENCE SUMMARY.
(Erase heading not required.)

Instructions regarding—War Diaries and Intelligence Summaries are contained in F.S. Regs., Part II. and the Staff Manual respectively. Title pages will be prepared in manuscript.

Place	Date	Hour	Summary of Events and Information	Remarks and references to Appendices
Battlefield	Mar 25		A quiet day	nil
	26		246 Bty. bombarded the craters, ae S2&6.5 (reference trench map 36cSW3) in conjunction with a battery of 4.5" Howitzers. A 18 pr. battery fired shrapnel along the enemy first and second lines to prevent the enemy from seeing the position of the mortars. In spite of a high wind, several direct hits on the craters were obtained.	nil
	27		On Y.46 Bty. front the enemy opened fire with his mortars. Our mortars replying he ceased firing.	nil
	28		A quiet day.	nil
	29		At the request of the infantry X.46 Bty. fired intermittently throughout the night on the craters opposite R.4.	nil
	30		Nothing to report.	nil
	31		A quiet day	nil

M.C. Grain
Capt. R.F.A.
i/c Trench Mortars
46th Divisional Artillery

CONFIDENTIAL

WAR DIARY.

MEDIUM TRENCH MORTAR BATTERIES - 46th: DIVISIONAL ARTILLERY

APRIL 1st: to 30th: 1916.

Army Form C. 2118.

WAR DIARY
or
INTELLIGENCE SUMMARY

(Erase heading not required.)

Instructions regarding War Diaries and Intelligence Summaries are contained in F. S. Regs., Part II. and the Staff Manual respectively. Title Pages will be prepared in manuscript.

Place	Date	Hour	Summary of Events and Information	Remarks and references to Appendices
Bustlefield	April 1		A quiet day.	N.B.Z.
	2.		A quiet day. Y46 Trench Mortar Battery registered on enemy front line.	N.B.Z
	3.		During the evening four guns of Y46 Battery fired forty rounds at the Sap at S.21.B.8.9 (reference map 36c S.W.3) and with support of an 18 pr. battery, on the trenches to the right of the sap. Several direct hits were obtained on the base of the sap and on the enemy's trenches. Immediately after the explosion of one of the bombs, a second and greater explosion took place, probably of an enemy grenade store. X46 Battery fired at and damaged the enemy front line.	N.B.Z.
	4.		X46 Battery fired several rounds at enemy trenches with success.	N.B.Z.
	5-6		A quiet day.	N.B.Z.
	7.		X46 Battery replied to the fire of hostile trench mortars, forcing them to stop firing.	N.B.Z.
	8.		X46 and Z46 Batteries both fired repeatedly on enemy trenches, X46 Battery being successful in knocking down parts of the enemy front line.	N.B.Z.
	9.		A quiet day.	N.B.Z.
	10.		Z46 Battery, with the support of 18 Pr. field guns, fired on an enemy mine shaft at S.28.9.9.9 (reference map 36c S.W.3) Several direct hits were obtained, considerable damage being done to the cement.	N.B.Z.

WAR DIARY
or
INTELLIGENCE SUMMARY

(Erase heading not required.)

Army Form C. 2118.

Place	Date	Hour	Summary of Events and Information	Remarks and references to Appendices
In the field	April 11.		Y 46 Battery fired on a sap at S.21.c.8.9 (reference map 36cS.W.?) with the support of 18 pr. Material was seen to be thrown into the air from the sap, so the damage done must have been considerable.	n.s.
	12.		X 46 and an 18 pr. battery combined in shelling the crater at A.7.7 (reference map 51BN.W.1) with success several bombs falling on the lip of the crater held by the enemy	n.s.
	13.		Y 46 Battery fired fifteen rounds at the enemy trenches. During the afternoon Z 46 Battery and a battery of 4.5" Howitzers shelled the trenches at S.28.a.7.4 (reference map 36cS.W.?) bursts repeatedly falling within two yards of enemy trenches, which were considerably damaged. The enemy fired on our mortar positions, but failed to do any damage, the majority of his 77 mm shrapnel bursting behind the position. Y 46 battery also fired 19 rounds at trench mortars.	n.s.
	14.		Y 46 Battery fired on the trenches at S.15.c (reference map 36cS.W.?) part of the trenches being blown in	n.s.
	15.		A quiet day Y 46 and Z 46 Batteries each fired a few rounds at enemy trenches and emplacements, Y 46 Battery succeeding in knocking down the enemy's parapet in one place	n.s.
	16.		A quiet day	n.s.

WAR DIARY or INTELLIGENCE SUMMARY

(Erase heading not required.)

Army Form C. 2118.

Place	Date	Hour	Summary of Events and Information	Remarks and references to Appendices
In the field	April 17		X46 Battery fired on enemy trenches. The enemy replied with 5.9" common shell, and succeeded in blowing in one of our mortar positions, but no material damage was done. Y46 Battery registered two mortars from a new position.	n/g/s
	18.		A quiet day.	n/g/s
	19.		Y46 Battery stood to the mortars all night at the request of the infantry but were not required to fire.	n/g/s
	20.21		A quiet day. Nothing to report.	n/g/s
	22		In reply to hostile trench mortar fire, Y46 Battery fired and were successful in stopping the enemy's fire.	n/g/s
	23.		On Y46 Battery's front four enemy mortars bombarded our front line, and Y46 Battery in reply did extensive damage to enemy front line, blowing in about fifteen yards of trenches. This caused the hostile mortars to stop firing. On night 23rd/24th by opening fire Y46 Battery caused the enemy to cease firing rifle grenades. On night of 23rd/24th the batteries of the 46th Division were relieved by batteries of the 5th Division. At 9.30 am of the 23rd X25, Y25, and Z25 Trench Mortar Batteries arrived by motor lorry at ACQ, and at night proceeded to the trenches. The reliefs were carried out as follows:— X25 T.M. Battery relieved Z46 Battery Y25 ,, ,, ,, X46 ,, Z25 ,, ,, ,, Y46 ,,	

WAR DIARY
or
INTELLIGENCE SUMMARY

Army Form C. 2118.

Place	Date	Hour	Summary of Events and Information	Remarks and references to Appendices
In the Field	April 23		On completion of relief X/46 and Z/46 Batteries proceeded to their rest billets as follows:— X/46 Battery to ECOIVRES. Z/46 Battery to CAMBLAIN L'ABBÉ. Owing to a sudden shortage of transport on the Light Railway at BRAY, Y/46 Battery could not obtain transport & were to return to rest billets on night 23rd/24th.	N.G.S.
	24		On night 24th/25th, Y/46 Battery returned to rest billets at CAMBLAIN L'ABBÉ.	N.G.S.
	25	9.30 a.m.	X/46, Y/46 and Z/46 Batteries proceeded by motor lorry to reserve billets at NEUVILLE AU CORNET.	N.G.S.
		10.0 a.m.	Capt. N.G. Strain, ℅ Trench Mortars 46th Divisional Artillery, handed over to Capt. J. Dudley, ℅ Trench Mortars 25th Divisional Artillery.	N.G.S.
	26-30		The Medium Trench Mortar Batteries commenced a course of training, a syllabus of which is attached.	N.G.S.

N.G. Strain
Captain R.S.A.
℅ Trench Mortars
46th Divisional Artillery.

Trench Mortars
46th Divisional Artillery.
Scheme of Training
April 23. 1916.

Per week.

__1 day (Sunday).__
9.0 – 11.0 a.m. Church Parade.
Afternoon Baths.

__3 days (Monday, Wednesday, Friday).__
8.30 – 9.0 a.m. Physical Training.
9.15 – 10.30 Route March.
11.0 – 12.0 Gun drill.
12.0 – 12.30 Practical Lecture.
2.0 – 3.0 Semaphore ⎱ Signalling.
3.30 – 4.30 Morse ⎰

__2 days (Tuesday, Thursday).__
8.30 – 9.0 Physical Training.
9.30 – 10.30 Gun drill.
11.0 – 12.0 Marching Drill.
12.15 – 12.45 Fatigues – overhauling and cleaning guns.
Afternoon Football – games.

__1 day (Saturday).__
8.30 – 9.0 Physical Training.
9.30 – 10.30 Gun drill.
11.0 – 11.45 Marching Drill.
12.0 – 12.45 Kit Inspection – Smoke helmet and respirator. Sword drill.
Afternoon Football – games.

__Lectures__ 6.30 p.m. to 7.0 p.m. – 3 per week.
__1st week.__ General discipline – construction and employment of Trench Mortars.
__2nd week.__ Employment of Trench Mortars. Types of ammunition and fuses employed. Selection and construction of positions.
__3rd week.__ Ranging. Mechanism and care of the rifle.
__4th week.__ Telephone working and wire laying. Grenades – construction.

M.C. Train.
Captain R.F.A
i/c Trench Mortars
46th Divisional Artillery.

CONFIDENTIAL

WAR DIARY.

MEDIUM TRENCH MORTAR BATTERIES.

May 1st: to 31st: 1918.

WAR DIARY or INTELLIGENCE SUMMARY

Army Form C. 2118.

Places	Date	Hour	Summary of Events and Information	Remarks and references to Appendices
In the field	May 1916			
	1-3		The Medium Trench Mortar Batteries were in training at NEUVILLE AU CORNET. Officer in charge of Trench Mortars and the officers of X46 Battery reconnoitred the trenches opposite FONQUEVILLERS and returned to NEUVILLE AU CORNET the same day.	NES
	3		X46 Battery proceeded by route to 48th Divisional Area from NEUVILLE AU CORNET and were billeted at POMMIER.	NES
	4		Y46 and Z46 Batteries proceeded with their scheme of training.	NES
	5-7		X46 Battery relieved X48 Trench Mortar Battery in trenches opposite FONQUEVILLERS. The relieving Battery took over pieces of FONQUEVILLERS. Y46 and Z46 Batteries moved by motor lorry into billets at BIENVILLERS AU BOIS.	NES
	8		Trench Mortar Batteries reconnoitred for gun emplacements and in the afternoon work was commenced on the positions selected.	NES
	9		Capt. R.E. Train R.F.A. took over from Lt. Col. Anderson, R.A. the office of Trench Mortars 48th Divisional Artillery. The construction of emplacements and dugouts in FONQUEVILLERS was commenced.	NES
	10		137/1 and 137/2 Trench Mortar Batteries ("B" Stokes) were attached to X46 Battery to assist in digging emplacements.	NES
	11		Z46 Battery had one man slightly wounded by an enemy trench mortar. Also work on the mortar emplacements.	NES
	12			NES

WAR DIARY or INTELLIGENCE SUMMARY

Army Form C. 2118.

Place	Date	Hour	Summary of Events and Information	Remarks and references to Appendices
In the field	1916 May 13-14.		Batteries proceeded with their work on emplacements.	M.S.Z.
	15.		138/1 and 138/2 Batteries were attached to Y 46 Battery, and 159/1 and 159/2 Z46 Battery to assist in digging emplacements.	M.S.Z.
	16-18		All batteries worked on their positions X46 and Z46 Batteries without any interruption, but Y46 on several occasions were forced to cease operations owing to the enemy trench-mortaring and shelling the locality in which the positions were being dug.	M.S.Z.
	19		Y46 and Z46 Batteries each moved one officer and the personnel of two gun detachments from (51) MILLERS AU BOIS into advanced bivouacs at PONQUEVILLERS.	
	20-27		Nothing of an unusual nature occurred & work proceeded without any serious interruption.	
	28		Y46 Battery were hindered by enemy shelling - in an endeavour to avoid a shell one man of this Battery Dr.Hy. Lunet. Ship. had some bars against. At the same time a man in Y46 Battery had his leg broken by a fall of earth from a bombproof. They have been evacuated.	
	29-31		Nothing of importance has occurred.	

E.J.Mawieth? R.F.A.
for O/C French Mortars
46 H D.A.

CONFIDENTIAL.

WAR DIARY.

HEAD QUARTERS

46th: MEDIUM TRENCH MORTAR BATTERIES.

JUNE 1st: to JUNE 30th: 1916.

WAR DIARY or INTELLIGENCE SUMMARY

Army Form C. 2118.

(Erase heading not required.)

Place	Date	Hour	Summary of Events and Information	Remarks and references to Appendices
In the field	JUNE 1-2		Nothing to report.	n.g.z
	3		During the afternoon Z/46 Battery ranged four guns on the enemy front line trenches. All the ranges were fired of which 720 were observed to be direct hits and to do considerable damage to the trenches.	n.g.z
	4		At midnight 3/4-6-16 Z/46 Battery opened fire on selected points of the enemy's front line, the firing being in conjunction with field batteries. Satisfactory rounds were fired altogether.	n.g.z
	5		Z/46 Battery fired mine rounds at enemy front line with success.	n.g.z
	6		X/46 and Z/46 Batteries each reconnoitred two reserve positions, and on the night 6/7 work was commenced on the sites selected.	n.g.z
	7		Two positions for Y/46 Heavy Trench Mortar Battery were reconnoitred.	n.g.z
	8		Work was commenced on the Heavy Trench Mortar Positions by an infantry fatigue party of 80 men, under the supervision of an officer from the Machine Gun Trench Mortar Batteries.	n.g.z
	9		One man of Z/46 Battery was accidentally wounded.	n.g.z
	10-18		Work was carried on actively in preparing and strengthening sec mortar positions and in preparing bombers in the reserve trenches in FONQUEVILLERS.	n.g.z
	19		A direct hit was obtained by an enemy trench mortar on a gun position of Y/46 Battery, but little damage was done.	n.g.z
	20		Y/46 Battery carried and took over billets in VIE NULLERS AU BOIS. Z/46 Battery commenced work on a new position on the night 20/21 inst.	n.g.z
	21		Infantry working parties were detailed for the new position of V/46 Battery.	n.g.z

WAR DIARY
or
INTELLIGENCE SUMMARY

(Erase heading not required.)

Army Form C. 2118.

Place	Date JUNE	Hour	Summary of Events and Information	Remarks and references to Appendices
South of BETHUNE	21.		X46 Batty had one O.R. killed and one O.R. wounded in FONQUEVILLERS by an enemy shell. An emplacement of Z46 Battery was damaged by shell fire. En's this road repaired on night 21/22nd inst.	nil
	22.		Y46 Battery during the afternoon captured two Germans on the LA BRAYELLE ROAD. These were handed over to the Infantry.	nil
	23.		Lieut. E.S. Davies of X46 Battery proceeded sick to hospital.	nil
	24.		Reference the attached Operation Order, X46, Y46, Z46 Batteries bombarded the enemy line as per the instructions for "U" Day.	nil
	25.		Ambulance was carried out as for "V" Day. Z46 Battery OP. position containing two guns was destroyed by shell fire. 3 O.R.s being killed. Lieut. R. Siddons and 4 O.R.s being wounded. Lieut. Siddons and 3 O.R.s proceeded to hospital, the remaining O.R. being placed under medical treatment regimentally.	nil
	26.		2/Lt. Plummer joined X46 Battery. Bombardment carried out as for "W" Day	nil
	27.		2/Lt. Athin proceeded to hospital. Z46 Battery accidentally wounded. 2/Lt. Plummer proceeded sick to hospital. Z46 Battery night position was seriously damaged by shell fire. Night bombardment carried out as for "X" Day.	nil
			Bombardment proceeded as for "Y" Day	
	28.		2/Lieut. Holmes proceeded sick to hospital. 2/Lieut. E. Smith took over command of X46 Battery.	nil
	29.		2/Lieut. Arrowsmith joined X46 Battery	nil

Army Form C. 2118.

WAR DIARY
or
INTELLIGENCE SUMMARY
(Erase heading not required.)

Instructions regarding War Diaries and Intelligence Summaries are contained in F. S. Regs., Part II. and the Staff Manual respectively. Title Pages will be prepared in manuscript.

Place	Date	Hour	Summary of Events and Information	Remarks and references to Appendices
In the field.	JUNE 28.		Y46 Battery came into action and commenced firing. Until July 1/1916 Y46 Battery shelled with considerable success the enemy trenches at selected points. This battery was successful in demolishing two houses, one of which contained enemy very light stores, which were ignited by the explosion of the heavy shells.	M.G.
	29.		2/Lieut. Neyton took over command of Z46 Battery. X46 Battery were heavily shelled, and one emplacement was damaged. Two O.R.s were wounded. Bombardment continued as for "Y" day.	M.G.
	30.		One man from "Y"46 Battery proceeded wounded to hospital. 2/Lieut. Pope: proceeded sick to hospital. Two men of Y46 Battery were wounded.	M.G.

M.G. Train
Capt. R.F.A.
i/c Trench Mortars
46th Divisional Artillery.

"U" Day
— 1 —
WIRE CUTTING.

AMMUNITION
ALLOTMENT

Y.46 Battery

  Will cut a lane 100 yards
wide across GOMMECOURT Road
E.28.c. 48.45

100 rounds.
N.F.

Z.46 Battery

  Will cut a lane 100 yards
wide opposite point E.28.b.7.5 and
a lane 60 yards wide opposite
little "Z" opposite E.28.c.35.20.

100 rounds
N.F.

X.46 Battery

  Will cut a lane 100 yards
wide end of Communication Trench
E.28.b.20.15

100 rounds
N.F.

NOTE The Trench Mortar and 18 pr.
Batteries will be given different times

  During wire cutting each day
X/46 and Y/46 Trench Mortar Batteries will
be placed under the Control of the Right
Group Commander, and Z/46 Trench Mortar
Battery under the control of the Left Group
Commander. The respective Group Commander
will be responsible for informing the Trench
Mortar Batteries exactly where any wire is
to be cut, other than that laid down in these
orders.

  All Wire Cutting will be carried out
in the closest Liaison with the Infantry,
Combined reconnaissance being carried out
for this purpose.

"V" Day

Wire cutting

		AMMUNITION ALLOTMENT
X 46 Battery)	Will cut wire between enemy's 1st: and 2nd: Lines the whole front of GOMMECOURT WOOD within range	
Y 46 Battery)		300 rounds N.F.
Z 46 Battery)	Will cut a LANE 100 yards wide opposite end of Communication Trench at E.23.C.55.47.	

X 46. Battery.		
Y.46. Battery.	Will engage Strong Points that they can reach.	100 D.F.
Z.46. Battery.		

"V" Day.

BOMBARDMENT "A"

2nd. Phase.
0.45 to 1-30.

At 0.45 all Batteries except Trench Mortars will lift their fire on to the enemy's 2nd: Line, firing "S.S" to begin with followed by H.E.

Trench Mortars will stop firing

3rd. Phase.

At 1.30 all Batteries except 4.5 Howitzers and Trench Mortars will turn their fire on to the same Zones as 1st Phase, and fire ____

Bombardment. "B" — 0.0. pm.

A similar Bombardment to that on "U" Night will be arranged by Group C.O's & O.C. Trench Mortar Batteries.

Ammunition Allowance. On Wire 150 rounds per Group Shrapnel.

Night Bombardment of Tracks etc. 100 rounds Shrapnel & 150 H.E per Group.

"W." Day

Wire Cutting

		Ammunition Allotment
X 46. Battery Y 46. Battery Z 46. Battery	Will cut Lanes for 100 yards on flanks of Wire cut on U day.	300. N.F
X 46. Battery Y 46. Battery Z 46. Battery V 46. Battery	Strong Points along the whole front System	"D.F" 30 30 30

1. mortar will fire from 0.0 to 1- on GOMMECOURT Village and 1 mortar will fire on Big "Z" Area.   20

Bombardment "A"

2nd Phase Infantry Advance.
0.30 to 1.

| X 46 Battery
Y 46 Battery
Z 46 Battery | GOMMECOURT VILLAGE and Strong Points in Big "Z". | 40 D.F.
Per Battery |

NOTES

(2) V. 46 Battery will fire an additional 60 rounds during the day, special attention to FORD Trench and LITTLE "Z".

"X" Day.

Wire Cutting

X.46. T.M. Battery.
Y.46. T.M. Battery. } Will concentrate on any wire not cut on front of 137th Inf Bde for 1st & 2nd Lines as reported by Infantry.
Z.46. T.M. Battery.

Ammunition Allotment
400 (A) & 100 (N.F) per Bty.

} Will concentrate on any wire not cut on front of 139th Inf Bde for 1st & 2nd Line as reported by Infantry.

400. A.
100. N.F
per Battery.

X. DAY BOMBARDMENT "A"
1st: PHASE O.15 a.45

X.46. T.M. Battery.
Y.46. T.M. Battery. } Same as 1st: Phase "V" Day and stop firing
Z.46. T.M. Battery.

50 rounds "D.F."
50 rounds D.F
50 rounds D.F"

V.46. Battery } GOMMECOURT Road Barrier and Strong Points in Big & Little "Z"   20 rounds.

3rd. Phase.
10.45 p.m.

Trench Mortars on points in Front Line Trenches.   25 rounds "D.F."

12.15 a.m.
Repeat the above.

INTENSE BOMBARDMENT

(1) 5.5 a.m to 5.45 a.m in cooperation with Smoke. Bombardment to increase in intensity during the last 15 minutes.

(2) 6.25 a.m to 7.5 a.m in cooperation with Corps Heavy Artillery and Smoke.
Bombardment to increase in intensity during last 15 minutes.

(3) The Medium & Heavy Trench Mortars will fire during these Bombardments on selected Strong Points & Trench Junctions within their range.

X.46
Y.46 } 50 rounds per Battery.   V.46.   40 rounds.
Z.46

V.46 will also fire during the day 20 rounds into GOMMECOURT village, and from the Barrier along the GOMMECOURT Road at points within range.

"Y" DAY

Wire Cutting

		Ammunition Allotment
X. 46. T.M Battery. Y. 46. T.M Battery.	Will concentrate on any wire not cut on front of 137th Inf Bde for 2nd and 3rd. Lines & GOMMECOURT WOOD	400. A. 100 (N.F) per Battery
Z. 46. T.M Battery.	Will concentrate on any wire not cut in front of 139th. Infantry Bde for 2nd. Line & N.W. corner of GOMMECOURT WOOD.	400.(A) 100 (N.F) per Battery

Should the Infantry Patrols report any wire not cut along the front line, the wire must be cut in addition on this day.

X. 46. T.M Battery. Y. 46. T.M Battery. Z. 46. T.M Battery.	Will complete destruction of works, Special attention being paid to trenches N. and S. of GOMMECOURT Road and along the Western edge of GOMMECOURT WOOD. Continue on Strong Points along the front system and the little Z	75 "D.F" per Battery
V. 46 Battery.	Will fire on Strong Points round the Barrier and GOMMECOURT Village and in the Big and Little "Z" area.	20 rounds

---

BOMBARDMENT "A"
2nd. Phase.
0.15 to 1-30

X 46 T.M Battery Y 46. T.M Battery Z 46. T.M Battery.	Same as for 1st. Phase but different points.	40 rounds "D.F" per Battery
V. 46. T.M Battery.	Same as for 1st. Phase but different points	20 rounds

In addition V/46 will fire 40 rounds during the day on to selected points within range, special attention being paid to GOMMECOURT Village & the Big Z. area.

"Y" Day.

Wire Cutting
3rd Phase. 2.30 - 3

4.5 Howitzers and Trench Mortars will not take part.

4th Phase.
10.30 P.M

With the exception of 4.5 Howitzers and Trench Mortars, each Battery will fire 3 rounds Gun Fire on Lines for 1st Phase, followed at 30 minutes interval by the same procedure on Lines for 2nd Phase.

This action will be repeated at 1 A.M.

Intense Bombardment

(1) 6.45 a.m. to 7.25 a.m. in co-operation with Smoke Bombardment to increase in intensity during last 15 minutes.
Both Groups same as (1) for "W" Day.
2" Trench Mortars   30 rounds per Battery.

(2) 4.45 p.m. to 5.25 p.m. in co-operation with Corps Heavy Artillery and Smoke. Bombardment to increase in intensity during last 15 minutes.

TIME TABLE

All Bombardments will be suspended from 4 to 4:30 pm daily up to "Y" Day inclusive to allow photographs to be taken. The fire will not continue after the times given, but if the ammunition is expended before the task completed, the allotted times for Rifle etc. Ammunition to be expended before the task completed, fire June etc.

DAY	DAY BOMBARDMENT	WIRE CUTTING	NIGHT BOMBARDMENTS	REMARKS
"U"	NIL	2" Trench Mortars 12 noon to 2 pm and 5 pm to 7:30 pm	9:30 pm to 3 am Tracks & Roads. Trenches not to unless wire that has been cut will be kept under intermittent fire.	(1) Group Commanders will arrange during wire cutting operations to engage observing Posts and to provoke enemy fire for Trench Mortars.
"V"	Registration to be continued except that 4 pm to 4:30 pm Bombardment "A" (1) 8:5 am to 8:50 am (2) 8:50 am to 10:35 am (3) 10:35 am	2" Trench Mortars 9 pm to 4 pm 5 pm to 4 pm	9:30 pm to 3 am As above	(1) It is more important to concentrate on the enemy's observing Posts when the 2" m are firing than when 18 pdrs are wire cutting.
"W"	Intense Bombardment "A" 9:45 am to 10:35 am Bombardment "A" (1) 6:30 pm to 7 pm (2) 7 pm to 7:30 pm (3) 8:15 pm	2" Trench Mortars 11 am to 1 pm 3 pm to 4 pm	Do	(2) Registration by Trench m must be of a desultory nature, as few Mortars as possible firing at the same time during registration. This is in order to mislead the enemy as to the no of Mortars actually available and their positions. Careful observation & ranging to ensure the Bombs falling inside the wire, is essential.
"X"	(1) Intense Bombardment 5:5 am to 5:45 am (2) Intense Bombardment 6:25 am to 7:10 am Bombardment "A" (1) 4:42 pm to 6:27 pm (2) 6:27 pm to 7:12 pm (3) 10:45 pm (4) 12:15 am	2" Trench Mortars 12 noon to 3 pm	Do	(3) All times unless strictly stated to contrary, will be strictly adhered to.
"Y"	Intense Bombardment (1) 6:45 am to 7:25 am (2) 4:45 pm to 5:35 pm Bombardment "A" (1) 9:20 am to 10:50 am (2) 10:5 am to 10:50 am (3) 11:50 am to 12:20 m (4) 1 pm			

TIME TABLE Y II Day.

Day Bombardments.	Wire Cutting.	Night Bombardments.
Intense Bombardment. 8-20 am to 9-15 am. To increase in intensity at 9-10 am. Left from 9.15 to 9.20 am. Bombardment "A" (1) 1-30 pm to 2.15 pm. (2) 2-15 pm to 3 pm. (3) 9.30 pm to 10 pm.	To arranged by Group Commander 9-30 A.M. to 1-30 p.m. And 4 p.m. to 7 p.m.	As for Y 1 day.

Particular attention will be paid to trenches which
photograph shews still undamaged.
N.O. firing to take place between 3.20 pm &
4 pm.

CONFIDENTIAL.

WAR DIARY.

46th: TRENCH MORTAR BATTERIES.

July 1st: to July 31st: 1916.

WAR DIARY or INTELLIGENCE SUMMARY

Army Form C. 2118.

(Erase heading not required.)

Place	Date	Hour	Summary of Events and Information	Remarks and references to Appendices
Souchez field	JULY 1		Y46, X46, Y46, Z46 Trench Mortar Batteries continued the bombardment as laid down in the attached Operation Order for "Z" Day. Z46 & section had one afterwards wounded. The single mortars of which each section Battery placed in a position safe for the intense bombardment immediately prior to the Infantry advance were quickly shelled out of action by the enemy, but the mortars were not damaged. Y46 battery during the night 1/2 not silenced two enemy machine guns.	
	2		Y46 and Z46 Batteries, together with one section of X46 and Y46 Batteries withdrew from action and proceeded to billets in FONQUEVILLERS.	
	3		The remaining sections of X46 and Y46 Batteries withdrew from action and all the Trench Mortar Batteries proceeded to billets in BIENVILLERS AU BOIS. Nothing to report.	
	4			
	5		X46, Y46, Z46 Batteries relieved in action Z57, X57, Y57 Batteries respectively. An exchange of guns was effected.	
	6-10		The Batteries were engaged in preparing positions.	
	11		X46, Y46, Y Batteries were relieved in action by X57, Z57 and X57, P Batteries respectively. Y46 Battery proceeded to BERLES AU BOIS and relieved Z46 Battery in action. One section of Y46 Battery proceeded to BERLES. X46, Z46 and one section of Y46 proceeded to billets in BELLACOURT.	

Army Form C. 2118.

WAR DIARY
or
INTELLIGENCE SUMMARY
(Erase heading not required.)

Instructions regarding War Diaries and Intelligence Summaries are contained in F. S. Regs., Part II. and the Staff Manual respectively. Title Pages will be prepared in manuscript.

Place	Date	Hour	Summary of Events and Information	Remarks and references to Appendices
Battle field	JULY 12.		Positions were reconnoitred for mortars of X46 and Z46 Batteries and in the evening work was commenced on these positions.	
	13.		Y46 Battery fired 45 rounds at the enemy wire cutting lanes through it successfully.	
	14.		X46 Battery proceeded to pieces in BIENVILLERS AU BOIS and relieved in action X37 and Y37 Battery. There was no exchange of guns.	
	15-M		Y46 Battery fired on the enemy front line.	
	16.		A quiet day.	
	17.		2/Lieut. B.S. Jones of Y46 Battery was attached to Z46 Battery.	
	18-28		Nothing to report. Batteries continued the preparation of positions.	
	24.		In reply to hostile trench mortar fire, X46 Battery fired on enemy front line. Three direct hits being obtained on the enemy trenches. This caused the hostile mortars to stop firing.	
	25.		Nothing to report.	
	26.		X46 Battery fired on enemy trenches with success.	
	27.		X46 Battery ranged on points on enemy trenches.	
	28.		X46 Battery fired on enemy wire and front line.	
	29-30		Nothing to report.	
	31.		X46 and Y46 Batteries fired on enemy wire and front line. Bands wide at 1½ fuze gave about 20% set in sheets but otherwise the shooting was successful.	

M.G. Baxain
Capt. R.F.A.
½ Trench Mortars.

— 65 to 0. **Z DAY.** Bombardment.

Unit	Date	Time	TASK	REMARKS	AMMUNITION ALLOTMENT
X.46 Battery Y.46 Battery Z.46 Battery		—65 to 0. 2 & 30 zero	Strong Points along the enemy's front system. The mortars in Saps 1 and 11 will open fire during this Bombardment, on the enemy's wire in front of 3rd line & west edge of GOMMECOURT WOOD. Mortars in Sap 4 will fire during this Bombardment on wire in front of NEW trench about the junctions with the OUSE and ORINOCO trenches and Points N. & S. of those junctions within range.	The mortars will engage FORD Trench. 2.46. will engage New Trench E 23.c.6.3 to E 23. c.5.1. in addition to other junction points.	Up to 80 rounds per Battery "D.F." and 25 rounds Newton Fuze Fn each mortar in 1, 2 & 4 Saps.
V.46. Battery.		—65 to 0. ZERO.	1 mortar to demolish trenches N & S of GOMMECOURT Road from E 28.c.75.30 to E 28.d.40.15 and Ford Trench. 1 mortar in trench junctions in area of Big 4 Little 2 special attention being paid to E. 23.c.6.1 & E 23.c.6.3		10 rounds per mortar. 10 rounds per mortar.
			1st Phase of attack.		
X.46 Battery Y.46 Battery		0.0 to 0.35	Strong Points in GOMMECOURT village & GOMMECOURT Chateau. Mortars in Sap 1 will fire 5 rounds on Gomm Court village. Mortars in Sap 4 will continue on the New Trench until 0.20 if necessary, firing D.F. Mortars in Sap 2 will not fire.	The Infantry will be advancing along the GOMM COURT Rd & wire front trenches for 70 yards S. of the road — Care must be taken not to endanger the Bombers.	Up to 50 rounds per Battery.
2.46. Battery. (Nr section)		0.0 to 0.35.	Strong Points in area of Big 2	The Infantry will bomb up to end of Trench E.23.c.45.30 Care must be taken not to endanger the Bombers	

1st. Phase of Attack - 0.0 to 0.35. (contd)

Unit	Date	Time	TASK	Remarks	Ammunition Allotment
V.46. Battery		0.0 to 0.35	1 Mortar on GOMMECOURT Village keeping 200 yards South of the road. 1 Mortar on area of B.19.2"Y" on points within range up to the junction of New Trench & PIGEON WOOD.	See Remarks for 2.46.B	up to 4 rounds per Mortar.
"X" "Y" & "Z" Trench Mortar Batteries.		0.35 to 3.	2nd. Phase of Attack 0.35 to 2.35 (Consolidation) The Mortar per Battery will be moved forward in support of Infantry. Remaining Mortars continue on previous objectives.		up to 100 rounds per Battery.
V.46. Battery.		0.35 to 3	As for previous Phase.		up to 40 rounds.

NOTES.

(a) Artillery lifts are based on the assumption that the 137th. Infantry Brigade will reach the F. edge of GOMMECOURT WOOD at 0.20 and advancing towards their second objective reaching Fill Trench at 0.30. 139th. Infantry Brigade capturing the enemy 2nd. line at 0.8 & advancing to capture the New Trench at 0.20.

(b) Fire will be kept up on GOMMECOURT village until 3 hours, when it will be switched on to GOMMECOURT PARK.

(c) Fire for all Batteries after 2.30 hours will be as necessary according to the situation.

CONFIDENTIAL.

WAR DIARY.

46th: Divisional Artillery Trench Mortar Batteries.

AUGUST 1st: to AUGUST 31st: 1916.

Army Form C. 2118.

WAR DIARY
or
INTELLIGENCE SUMMARY

(Erase heading not required.)

Instructions regarding War Diaries and Intelligence Summaries are contained in F. S. Regs., Part II. and the Staff Manual respectively. Title Pages will be prepared in manuscript.

Place	Date	Hour	Summary of Events and Information	Remarks and references to Appendices
In the field	August 1		X46 Battery fired on enemy line and trenches 61 rounds and Y46 Battery 26 rounds, doing considerable damage to the wire and enemy trenches. One round from X46 Battery was observed to blow up a number of logs and bags out of the enemy's front line. Field A.S.A. at Righfort fired Z46 Battery from 335 15:06. F.D.A.	nil
	2.		X46 Battery fired 30 rounds on the enemy front line wire opposite MONCHY, and Y46 Battery 23 rounds on the opposing trenches.	nil
	3.		X46 Battery fired 28 rounds on front line wire and Y46 Battery 3 rounds. The wire was badly damaged.	nil
	4.		X46 and Y46 Batteries fired altogether 72 rounds on the enemy trenches with success. During the afternoon Y46 Battery ranged on prominent points in MONCHY with 10 rounds, one of which blew up a house.	nil
	5.		Y46 Battery fired 25 rounds into MONCHY during the afternoon and evening. Delays were caused on several occasions by shell jamming in the bore of the gun. X46 Battery fired 17 rounds at enemy wire and Y46 Battery 112 rounds at enemy wire and front line. A great amount of damage was done to both wire and front line with the repeated bombardments. Y46 Battery cut a lane about 20 yards wide through the wire.	nil
	6.		Y46 Battery on night 5/6 fired a further 32 rounds on enemy trenches	nil

Army Form C. 2118.

WAR DIARY
or
INTELLIGENCE SUMMARY

(Erase heading not required.)

Instructions regarding War Diaries and Intelligence Summaries are contained in F. S. Regs., Part II. and the Staff Manual respectively. Title Pages will be prepared in manuscript.

Place	Date August	Hour	Summary of Events and Information	Remarks and references to Appendices
In the field	7		V46 Battery light gun fired 5 rounds on enemy trenches opposite 167th Infantry Brigade front. No direct hits were obtained. There was no reply.	
	8			
	9		V46 Battery fired 9 rounds and Y46 Battery 15 rounds at the same target on the 7th of linen. After one direct hit from V46 Battery a large quantity of speech & ground now was rising from the enemy trench. No additional explosion was heard. Gun's Co-operated. Small arms fire used by the enemy. One section from 1/6 Medium Trench Mortar Battery was withdrawn from action & left in billets. Guns of such were ordered to form a nucleus to be employed for the purposes of special concentrations on the Divisional front.	
	10		The machine gun sections of X46 and Y46 Batteries ranged from BIENVILLERS and BERLES respectively against villages in BELLACOURT, a concentration against the "BLOCKHOUSE" was carried on interfering positions on the 167th Infantry Brigade front.	
	11-13		A concentration of the "BLOCKHOUSE" took place in conjunction with other batteries. 165 rounds were fired. No reply from the enemy.	
	14		V46 Battery in addition fired 5 rounds, most of which were observed as O.K. This was one of a few places which were the subject of the medium Batts fire.	
	15		BELLACOURT was fired in BERLES and commenced in preparation positions at 12.78 and started stray shells on the preparation with a view to concealing and of positions.	
	16-18			

WAR DIARY or INTELLIGENCE SUMMARY

Army Form C. 2118.

Place	Date	Hour	Summary of Events and Information	Remarks and references to Appendices
In the field	August 19		A bombardment of an enemy Battery in 15 to Infantry Brigade area took place, 16 rounds were fired, the majority of which were effective. A stokes gun position of 246 Battery was ranged on by the enemy. The position being damaged and one officer and one man wounded. 246 to Battery's position on firing the 1st of one 6 inch again brought the enemy's fire onto their own & the front of the pits without damage. The presence of trench mortars in the fire necessitated the guns standing from firing until the explosive could be rendered inert and then removed.	nil
	20.		The mobile sections withdrew from action to BERLES.	nil
	21.		One section each of X46, Y46, Z46 Batteries moved from billets in BERLES to BELLACOURT.	nil
	22.		Preparations were made for a bombardment against the "BLOCKHOUSE".	nil
	23.		Six 2" Mortars bombarded the "BLOCKHOUSE" and shelled the enemy mine system & land to the N. of the "BLOCKHOUSE" through the wire. The enemy trenches were considerably damaged; the ammunition expenditure was 175 rounds.	nil
	24.		During the night Z46 Battery fired 10 rounds into the "BLOCKHOUSE". The mobile sections of Z 2" Batteries marched from BELLACOURT to BERLES.	nil

Army Form C. 2118.

WAR DIARY
or
INTELLIGENCE SUMMARY
(Erase heading not required.)

Place	Date	Hour	Summary of Events and Information	Remarks and references to Appendices
In the field	August 30		The mobile section of the machine batteries prepared positions in 157th and 158th Infantry Brigade fronts.	
	31		X 46 Battery cut a lane in enemy wire with 64 rounds of ammunition. The wire was completely cut to a breadth of 20 yards. X 46 Battery fired 60 rounds into enemy trenches. Fire rounds were effective, the remaining ones falling between our front line and the enemy's.	

M. G. Strain
Lt. Col. R.F.A.
C/ Brigade Major
46 Divisional Artillery.

CONFIDENTIAL.

WAR DIARY.

Trench Mortar Batteries.
46 Div Arty:

SEPTEMBER 1st: to SEPTEMBER 30th: 1916.

WAR DIARY or INTELLIGENCE SUMMARY

Army Form C. 2118.

Place	Date	Hour	Summary of Events and Information	Remarks and references to Appendices
In the field	SEPTEMBER 1.		Nothing to report.	
	2.		Seven 2" trench mortars took part in a combined bombardment with other Artillery against an enemy salient opposite 137th Infantry Brigade front. From 5.0 p.m. to 8.30 p.m. the mortars shelled the enemy wire. Two lanes were completely cut through the wire, one about 6 yards wide and the other about 30 yards wide. Sure shunning lanes were also cut through the enemy wire. From 8.30 p.m. to 11.30 p.m. the mortar bombarded the enemy trenches with considerable success. 315 rounds were fired altogether. A 4 point shrapnel lit the fuze of one bomb as the detachment were leaving the pit, point of attack charging the gun. The bomb exploded, the pit being wrecked, the other task being killed and one wounded. The gun was unlamaged.	NCZ
			Nothing to report.	NCZ
	10.		A bombardment of the enemy trenches took place at night. 6'5 rounds were fired but the result of the shooting could not be observed owing to the darkness.	NCZ
	11.		Medium trench mortar batteries were engaged in preparing emplacements.	NCZ
5–7				
	8.		In the afternoon a section of Y 46 battery fired 60 rounds on the enemy with much considerable success. The enemy retaliated with a few rounds from a 4.2 cm. and 2.7 cm. specific. A round of X 46 battery opened up to the R.A.C. of June.	NCZ
	9.		In the early morning a section of X 46 and Y 46 batteries fired together 29 rounds into enemy trenches doing much damage but drawing little retaliation.	NCZ

WAR DIARY
or
INTELLIGENCE SUMMARY

Army Form C. 2118.

Place	Date SEPTEMBER	Hour	Summary of Events and Information	Remarks and references to Appendices
In the field.	9.		From 4.0 p.m. to 5.0 p.m. 2 mortars of X46 Battery and one each from Y46 and Z46 Batteries engaged points on the enemy front line in 138th Infantry Brigade area. 160 rounds were fired in all. On several occasions sandbags and timber were thrown up from the enemy trenches. A concrete machine-gun emplacement was engaged, but could not be broken up, setting direct hits were obtained, as the bombs could not get any penetration.	M.E.D.
	10.		The mobile sections of X46, Y46 and Z46 Batteries moved their guns to BERLES, and then proceeded to billets in BELLACOURT.	M.E.D.
	11-18		Batteries were engaged in preparing positions on 137th and 138th Infantry Brigade fronts.	M.E.D.
	19.		Y46 Battery fired on enemy trenches and wire on 137th Infantry Brigade during the afternoon. Direct hits on enemy trenches were frequently obtained, and two gaps cut in the wire, permitting a raiding party to enter enemy trenches on night 19/20th Inst. During the night 2 guns of Y46 Battery barraged enemy front line and gaps for 50 minutes. Z46 Battery bombarded enemy trenches with one gun. Ammunition expenditure 237 rounds. Y46 Battery placed a 9.45" mortar in position on 137th Infantry Brigade front.	M.E.D.
	20.		Nothing to report.	M.E.D.
	21.		Commencing at 2.0 p.m. Z46 Battery, and the mobile sections of X46 and Y46 Batteries were engaged in cutting wire and bombarding the enemy front line opposite LATREVILLE. These operations continued until 7.10 p.m. with great success	M.E.D.

WAR DIARY or INTELLIGENCE SUMMARY

Army Form C. 2118.

Place	Date SEPT.	Hour	Summary of Events and Information	Remarks and references to Appendices
In the field.	22		The wire being completed and the backs of a German being found afterwards in the hostile trenches. At 12.15 am 22-9-16 four 2"S trench Mortars bombarded the enemy front line, continuing until 1"5 am. Ammunition expended 678 rounds. At about 6.30 pm a shell burst at the front of one of the gun-pits, bringing the gun and wounding two men.	M.G. To
	23		The mobile section of X46, Y46 and Z46 stands withdrew from action in BELLACOURT and moved into billets in BEAMETZ.	M.G. To
	24-25 26		Work was carried out on positions opposite MONCHY. Nothing to report.	M.G. To
			One 9.45" mortar fired 9 rounds onto enemy trenches opposite the work of RANSART. Three rounds were effective in the enemy trenches and one round was abnormally short falling about ten yards in front of the gun-pit. The fuze of this bomb failed to arm, however. English ammunition was used. Nothing to report.	M.G. To
	27 28		Y46 Battery fired 4 rounds and Z46 Battery 3 rounds, ranging on new targets.	M.G. To
	24-30		Work was carried out on Mortar Emplacements.	M.G. To

M.G. _____
Captain R.T.A
D. O. T. M.
46th Divisional Artillery

CONFIDENTIAL.

WAR DIARY.

HEAVY AND MEDIUM TRENCH MORTAR BATTERIES.

October 1st: to October 31st: 1916.

****

WAR DIARY
or
INTELLIGENCE SUMMARY

Trench Mortars — G.S. Divisional Artillery

(Erase heading not required.)

Army Form C. 2118.

Place	Date	Hour	Summary of Events and Information	Remarks and references to Appendices
In the field	OCTOBER 1		Z46 Battery fired 5 rounds ranging at enemy trenches.	nil
	2.		Y46 Battery fired 4 rounds.	nil
	3.		Batteries were engaged in preparing positions for future wire-cutting operations.	nil
	4.		In reply to hostile mortar fire Y46 Battery fired 22 rounds with success at enemy trenches.	nil
	5.		During the afternoon the mobile section of Batteries fired on enemy wire and trenches opposite MONCHY with considerable success. One gap was cut through the wire about 20 yards wide, and one about 2–3 yards wide. A dugout in the enemy front line was blown up. Ammunition expended 618 rounds. During these operations the enemy obtained two hits on our mortar emplacements, wounding three men. Y46 Battery fired 5 rounds into MONCHY, one of which was successful in hitting a house.	
	6.		Y46 Battery fired 12 rounds at enemy front line. Z46 Battery fired 15 rounds at enemy trenches in reply to hostile mortar fire. The enemy mortars were silenced.	nil
	7.		Y46 Battery fired 34 rounds on the enemy front line. A direct hit on a 4'2" shell was obtained on an gun pit, with one damaging personnel of gun. Z46 Battery fired 3 rounds.	nil
	8.		With the mobile section of X46 and Y46 Batteries fired on enemy trenches and wire opposite BLAIREVILLE. 358 rounds being fired. At 2.0 p.m. Z46 Battery with the mobile section of X46 and Y46 Batteries continued wire cutting and bombarding the enemy. 266 rounds were fired. The wire was	nil

WAR DIARY

Trench Mortars of 46 Divisional Artillery

INTELLIGENCE SUMMARY

(Erase heading not required.)

Army Form C. 2118.

Place: In the field.

Date	Hour	Summary of Events and Information	Remarks and references to Appendices
OCTOBER 8 (contd)		cut were successfully in places, the other gap being not so good. One N.C.O. was wounded by the premature bursting of a bomb. During the night 8/9 the enemy trenches were bombarded for 27 minutes by five medium mortars.	n/a
9.		Y46 Battery sent every available man to billets in FONQUEVILLERS to dig a trench mortar emplacement.	n/a
10.		The mobile sections of X46, Y46, and Z46 Batteries withdrew from action opposite BLAIREVILLE and proceeded to billets in BERLES.	n/a
11. 12.		2/Lieut. W.B.C. Engwater was slightly wounded, 2 men of Y46 Battery were accidentally wounded. In the afternoon Y46 Battery fired in reply to enemy mortars. Several hits were obtained on the enemy trenches. Nothing to report.	n/a n/a
13. 14.		The detachments of Y46 Battery at FONQUEVILLERS returned to billets in BERLES. Three men of Z46 Battery and one man of Y46 Battery were wounded by enemy shell fire.	n/a n/a
15-16		2/Lieut. Reade went sick to hospital. X46 Battery and the mobile section of Y46 and Z 46 Batteries prepared for an operation opposite MONCHY in 138 Infantry Brigade area. 2/Lieut. Chapman joined X46 Battery.	n/a
17. 18		X46 Battery and the mobile section of Z46 Battery fired alarm the afternoon on enemy to North and South of MONCHY. Wire was considerable damaged and the enemy trenches were also repeatedly hit. From 8.30pm to 9.0pm three guns of Y46 Battery also fired on enemy wire and trenches. Ammunition fired 286 rounds. 2/Lieut. B. Smith of X46 Battery was wounded and proceeded to hospital. 2/Lieut. W.A.C. Engwater went to hospital on account of a nervous breakdown obtained from sickness. Shell fire on 11-10-16.	n/a n/a

Army Form C. 2118.

WAR DIARY
INTELLIGENCE SUMMARY
Trench Mortars of 46th Divisional Artillery

(Erase heading not required.)

Instructions regarding War Diaries and Intelligence Summaries are contained in F. S. Regs, Part II. and the Staff Manual respectively. Title Pages will be prepared in manuscript.

Place	Date	Hour	Summary of Events and Information	Remarks and references to Appendices
In the field	OCTOBER 19		Lieut. W. Gilbuis joined from 232 R. Brigade R.F.A. to command X.46 V.Battery. Lieut. B. J. Pepper joined Y.46 V.Battery from 46 D.A.C. Lieut. C. Wade joined Z.46 Battery from 231 Brigade R.F.A. The mobile sections withdrew from action opposite MONCHY and commenced preparations for an operation on 152 Infantry Brigade front.	M.G.
	20		Y.46 Battery fired 2 rounds against an enemy M.G. emplacement, but then had to cease firing on account of erratic shooting.	M.G.
	21		Y.46 Battery fired 48 rounds against enemy trenches with satisfactory results, the trenches being hit in several places.	M.G.
	22		The mobile sections of X.46 and Y.46 Batteries fired 93 rounds against enemy wires, and Z.46 Battery 20 rounds against enemy trenches.	M.G.
	23		X.46 and Z.46 Battery mobile sections fired 37 rounds against wire, and Z.46 Battery 14 rounds against trenches.	M.G.
	24		The mobile sections of X.46 and Z.46 Batteries and Y.46 Battery fired 104 rounds at wire.	M.G.
	25		Z.46 Battery fired 20 rounds at enemy trenches with good effect. Y.46 Battery and mobile section of X.46 Battery fired 317 rounds at enemy wire. The wire was very badly damaged, and being cut in two places. This firing drew forth considerable retaliation from hostile minenwerfer, which caused considerable annoyance but did little damage.	M.G.
	26		The mobile sections of Batteries withdrew from action to BERLES.	M.G.
	27		Nothing to report.	M.G.
	28		The mobile section of Z.46 Battery at CROISILLES rejoined its Battery.	M.G.

Army Form C. 2118.

WAR DIARY

or Intelligence Summary

Sprenchleoate of 46th Divisional Artillery

(Erase heading not required.)

Place	Date	Hour	Summary of Events and Information	Remarks and references to Appendices
In the field	OCTOBER 28 (contd)		From 3pm to 4pm one round of 2.46 battery fired 20 rounds against the "BLOCKHOUSE". Hits were obtained on their advance trench. X46 Battery also fired 4 rounds at the same time. One round fell abnormally short but the other three were good. No hit was obtained on the enemy trenches but two fell further 30 yards of a junction in hostile communication trenches.	MG
	29		Nothing to report.	MG
	30		The whole section of X46 and Y46 Batteries moved to Batteries in GROSVILLE.	MG
	31		Work was commenced in preparation for an operation against enemy trenches in front of BLAIREVILLE.	MG

M.G. Train
Capt. R.F.A.
D.O.T.M.
46th Divisional Artillery

~~Secret.~~
~~CONFIDENTIAL~~

WAR DIARY

46TH. DIVISIONAL ARTILLERY
TRENCH MORTARS

November 1916.

Army Form C. 2118.

Trench Mortar Batteries – 46th Divisional Artillery

WAR DIARY
INTELLIGENCE SUMMARY

(Erase heading not required.)

Place	Date	Hour	Summary of Events and Information	Remarks and references to Appendices
BAVINCOURT.	NOVEMBER 1-2. 3		Nothing to report. From 1.10 p.m. to 2.30 p.m. Six 2" mortars from Z46 Battery and the mobile section of X46 Battery fired on enemy front line opposite BLAIREVILLE. 221 rounds were fired, the enemy trenches being damaged; one wire obstacle and 150 yards of the hostile trenches.	nil
	4.		The mobile sections of X46 and Y46 Batteries withdrawn from action at G. ROSSVILLE.	nil
	5-8		Preparations were made for a bombardment against the "BLOCKHOUSE".	nil
	9.		In reply to the fire of an enemy minenwerfer, one mortar of Z46 Battery fired 15 rounds against the enemy trenches.	nil
	10		Nothing to report.	nil
	11		During the afternoon in conjunction with field batteries Z46 Battery fired 93 rounds against the "BLOCKHOUSE" damaging considerably a section of enemy trenches. The mobile sections of X46 and Y46 Batteries moved into billets in BERLES. 2/Lieut. D. A. Pepper of 46 D.A.C. attached Y46 Battery proceeded sick to hospital.	nil
	12.		From 2.30 am to 5.0 am in support of a release of gas against the enemy trenches Y46 Battery fired 15 rounds, the results being unobserved owing to the darkness.	nil
	13.		Y46 Battery fired 31 rounds against enemy mine South of RANSART damaging the mine. Z46 Battery registered on the opposition of the 148 Inft. Bde. Y46 Battery were in action for one hour and in addition enemy trenches several direct hits being obtained.	nil
	14			nil
	15			nil

Army Form C. 2118.

WAR DIARY

Trench Mortar Batteries - 48th Divisional Artillery

INTELLIGENCE SUMMARY

(Erase heading not required.)

Instructions regarding War Diaries and Intelligence Summaries are contained in F. S. Regs., Part II. and the Staff Manual respectively. Title Pages will be prepared in manuscript.

Place	Date	Hour	Summary of Events and Information	Remarks and references to Appendices
SAVINCOURT/G	NOVEMBER			
	17		During the day Y46 battery fired 25 rounds against enemy wire and Z46 battery 9 rounds against enemy trenches. No other batteries did accurate shooting.	M46
	18		Y46 battery continued its wirecutting operations.	M46
			Z46 battery fired 10 rounds registering on the TALUS.	
	19		Y46 battery fired 7 rounds against wire near PLANSART.	M46
	20		Y46 battery continued firing, the wire being damaged	M46
	21		Nothing to report.	M46
	22		Y46 battery carried on their operations against the enemy wire.	M46
			A continuation bombardment of enemy trenches and wire was carried out by 3 mortars of Y46 battery, 120 rounds were fired and much damage has been done to the enemy trenches. Part of the 2nd line 48th Divisional Artillery was taken over by the 48th Divisional Artillery relieving X46 battery. Y46 battery fired 16 rounds at enemy wire keeping the gap open.	M46
	23			M46
	24		Three 2" mortars were exchanged for 3 from trench mortar school. Y46 battery fired 144 rounds against the enemy wire. X46 battery fired 144 rounds against two points in enemy front line. On account of a high wind, the shooting was not as accurate as can normally be done.	M46
	25		X46 battery fired 45 rounds against enemy wire in continuance of the operations of 24-11-16.	M46
	26		X46 battery continued firing against enemy wire, firing 18 rounds. The wire was greatly damaged and object 6/15 were obtained on the front line.	M46
	27		Z46 battery fired one report against enemy observation post silencing it. Continued shell wire-cutting operations.	M46

2449 Wt. W14957/M90 750,000 1/16 J.B.C. & A. Forms/C.2118/12.

Army Form C. 2118.

WAR DIARY

Trench Mortar Batteries – 46th Divisional Artillery

INTELLIGENCE SUMMARY

(Erase heading not required.)

Place	Date	Hour	Summary of Events and Information	Remarks and references to Appendices
LAVINCOURT	NOVEMBER 28.		In combination with machine guns and Stokes Mortars, Z46 Battery fired 35 rounds into enemy front line opposite BLAIREVILLE. This operation was a complete success.	
	29.		X46 Battery fired into enemy wire to the N. of MONCHY. A lane is now cut through the wire.	
	30.		Y46 Battery fired 50 rounds against enemy trenches and wire, and X46 Battery 44 rounds.	

M.E. Groton
Capt. R.F.A
D.O.T.M.
46th Divisional Artillery

Secret

CONFIDENTIAL.

--:--:--

WAR   DIARY.

--:--:--

Trench Mortar Batteries.

--:--:--:--

December 1st: to December 31st: 1916.

WAR DIARY
or
INTELLIGENCE SUMMARY

Army Form C. 2118.

~~Trench Mortar Batteries~~ 4th Divisional Artillery
(Erase heading not required.)

Place	Date	Hour	Summary of Events and Information	Remarks and references to Appendices
BAVINCOURT.	DECEMBER 1-2.		Nothing to report.	n/c
	3.		Trench Mortar Batteries of 30th Divisional Artillery relieved X/46, Y/46, Z/46 and V/46 Batteries in action. 2" mortars were handed over & corresponding number being taken over at HUMBERCAMP from 30th Division. The heavy and medium Batteries moved from billets in GROSVILLE and BERLES into billets in HUMBERCAMP, and commenced a systematic training, the scheme of which is attached.	n/c
	4.			n/c
	10.		Batteries moved by train from SAULTY to LIGNY ST. FLOCHEL and commenced a course of instruction there at the School of Mortars 3rd Army.	n/c
HENU	19.		One half of the personnel of V/46, X/46, Y/46 and Z/46 Batteries of 4th Div. Arty. relieved in action Batteries of the 40th Div. Arty. The remaining personnel of V/46, X/46, Y/46 and Z/46 Batteries moved from LIGNY to SOUASTRE.	n/c
	20.		Batteries moved from LIGNY to SOUASTRE. Batteries moved into billets as follows:- V/46 and Z/46 Batteries at SOUASTRE. X/46 and Y/46 Batteries at BIENVILLERS-AU-BOIS.	n/c
	22-28.		Batteries were engaged in repairing and constructing positions.	n/c
	29.		Y/46 Battery in conjunction with 4.5" Howitzers fired 52 rounds against enemy trenches opposite MONCHY, with very good effect.	n/c

Army Form C. 2118.

WAR DIARY
or
INTELLIGENCE SUMMARY
Trench Mortar Batteries — 46th Divisional Artillery
(Erase heading not required.)

Instructions regarding War Diaries and Intelligence Summaries are contained in F. S. Regs., Part II. and the Staff Manual respectively. Title Pages will be prepared in manuscript.

Place	Date	Hour	Summary of Events and Information	Remarks and references to Appendices
HENU	December 30.		2.46 Battery fired 17 rounds against enemy front line wire, and 4.6 Battery 9 rounds against his trenches. None of these rounds being effective.	
	31		Nothing to report.	

M. E. Spratt
Capt. R.F.A.
½ Trench Mortars
46th Divisional Artillery

46th: DIVISIONAL ARTILLERY.

TRENCH MORTAR BATTERIES.

TRAINING SCHEME.

FIRST WEEK 4/12/16 to 10/12/16.

(1). SUNDAY.

    9-0 am.   INSPECTION.
    9-30 am.   CHURCH PARADE.
   11-30 am.   INSPECTION OF BILLETS.
   AFTERNOON. BATHS.

1 DAY (MONDAY).

8-30 am.   CLEANLINESS INSPECTION.
8-30 to 9am. PHYSICAL TRAINING.
9-15 to   ) SMOKE HELMET DRILL AND INSPECTION.
10-0 am.   )
10-15 to) KIT INSPECTION.
11-15 am.)
11-30 to) CLEANING OF GUNS.
12-30 pm.)
AFTERNOON. GENERAL CLEAN UP OF BILLETS.

2 DAYS. (TUESDAY AND THURSDAY).

8-30 to   ) PHYSICAL TRAINING.
9-0 am.   )
9-15 to   ) RIFLE AND MARCHING DRILL.
10-45 am.)
11-0 to   ) 2" BATTERIES - CLEANING OF GUNS.
12-15 pm.) 9-45" BATTERY - SEMAPHORE.
12-15 to) SMOKE HELMET DRILL AND INSPECTION.
12-45 pm.)
AFTERNOON. GAMES.
6 to   ) LECTURE.
6-45 pm.   )

2 DAYS. (WEDNESDAY AND FRIDAY.)

8-30 to   ) PHYSICAL TRAINING.
9-0 am.   )
9-15 to   ) RIFLE AND MARCHING DRILL.
10-45 am.)
11-0 to   ) 2" BATTERIES - GUN-DRILL.
12-0 pm.   ) 9-45" BATTERY - SEMAPHORE SIGNALLING.
2-0 to   ) 2" BATTERIES - SEMAPHORE SIGNALLING.
3-0 pm.   ) 9-45" BATTERY - GUN-DRILL ON 2" MORTARS.
3-0 to   ) LECTURE.
4-0 pm.   )

1 DAY. (SATURDAY).

8-30 to   ) PHYSICAL TRAINING.
9-0 am.   )
9-15 to   ) INSPECTION - (Full Marching Order with Pack).
10-0 am.   )
10-15 to) KIT INSPECTION.
12 Noon.   )
12-15 to) SMOKE HELMET DRILL.
12-45 pm.)

/Continued.

Continued 2.
----

(2). Marching Drill will invariably be carried out in full marching Order, with packs. It will also include at least ½ hour saluting drill.

(3). LECTURES. (FIRST WEEK - 5).
- (1). GENERAL DISCIPLINE.
- (2). GENERAL DISCIPLINE.
- (3). TRENCH MORTAR SERVICES.
- (4). MORTAR AND AMMUNITION.
- (5). RIFLE AND RIFLE MECHANISMS.

Captain R.F.A.
D.O.T.M. 46th Divisional Artillery.

December 1st 1916.

O.C's.
V/46 Trench Mortar Battery.
X/46 Trench Mortar Battery.
Y/46 Trench Mortar Battery.
Z/46 Trench Mortar Battery.
Office Copy.

CONFIDENTIAL.

WAR DIARY.

TRENCH MORTAR BATTERIES.

JANUARY 1st: to JANUARY 31st: 1917.

****

Army Form C. 2118.

Trench Mortar Batteries or 46th Divisional Artillery

WAR DIARY
INTELLIGENCE SUMMARY
(Erase heading not required.)

Instructions regarding War Diaries and Intelligence Summaries are contained in F.S. Regs., Part II. and the Staff Manual respectively. Title Pages will be prepared in manuscript.

Place	Date	Hour	Summary of Events and Information	Remarks and references to Appendices
HENU	JANUARY 1916			
	1-2		Nothing to report.	nil
	3		Simple to hostile minenwerfer fire, V46 Battery fired one round against the enemy's emplacement. Hostile fire was immediately stopped. Z46 Battery registered two mortars on enemy front line.	nil
	4		Nothing to report	nil
	5		V46 Battery fired 34 rounds onto enemy mortar positions and dugouts behind GOMMECOURT WOOD. The shooting was very accurate, one dugout being blown up and a large amount of R.E. material. Z46 Battery fired in reply to hostile minenwerfer fire, successfully silencing the enemy.	nil
	6		Z46 Battery fired 20 rounds against enemy front line with good effect. V46 Battery fired 36 rounds against a section of enemy trench. One dugout and three dugouts were blown up.	nil
	7-8		Work was continued in repairing and constructing mortar emplacements.	nil
	9		V46 Battery fired 31 rounds against hostile trench mortar emplacements. One round was almost directly short and another one blew up one of the enemy dumps. A V46 Battery was killed and one wounded by a 7.7 mm shell.	nil
	10		Z46 Battery fired 89 rounds and V46 acted 9 rounds against enemy trenches with good effect.	nil
	11		One man of V46 Battery wounded by 7.7 mm shell.	nil

2449 Wt. W14957/Mgo 750,000 1/16 J.B.C. & A. Forms/C2118/12.

WAR DIARY / INTELLIGENCE SUMMARY

Army Form C. 2118.

Trench Mortar Batteries 46th Divisional Artillery

(Erase heading not required.)

Instructions regarding War Diaries and Intelligence Summaries are contained in F.S. Regs., Part II. and the Staff Manual respectively. Title Pages will be prepared in manuscript.

Place	Date	Hour	Summary of Events and Information	Remarks and references to Appendices
HENU	JAN 13. 1917		Y 46 Battery fired 4 rounds at an enemy trench junction, one round being effective.	
	14.		Z 46 Battery fired on enemy trenches opposite GOMMECOURT in counter offensive to enemy minenwerfer fire.	
	15.		Y 46 Battery fired 11 rounds at an enemy strong point, some causing R.E. material.	
	16.		Y 46 Battery fired 24 rounds against Battery emplacements and support line. Z 46 Battery fired 25 rounds against this front and support line. The firing of both batteries was good and appeared very effective.	
	17.		Y 46 and Z 46 Batteries together fired 25 rounds and 46 Battery 2 rounds in counter offensive to enemy mortar fires causing the enemy to cease firing.	
	18.		Z 46 Battery fired 55 rounds against enemy front and support line at GOMMECOURT effectively. Y 46 Battery fired in reply to enemy mortar fire on mortar firing the East Tunnel.	
	19.		Y 46 Battery registered one mortar on new targets. V 46 Battery fired on enemy support line S. of MONCHY obtaining two hits. Y 46 Battery also fired on enemy front line.	
	20. 21.			
	22-26		3 O.P.s were continued by all batteries on that enemy cases	
	27.		Y 46 Battery fired 10 rounds on an enemy trench junction. One round blew up a quantity of stores and one round was a near short. The shots did me damage	
			Z 46 Battery fired 51 rounds on hostile support line.	

WAR DIARY
Trench Mortar Batteries — or 46th Divisional Artillery
INTELLIGENCE SUMMARY

Army Form C. 2118.

Place	Date	Hour	Summary of Events and Information	Remarks and references to Appendices
HENU.	JAN 1917 20. 21.		T.46.B. Battery fired 5 rounds into enemy trenches. Nothing to report.	1 M.S. 1 B.S.

M.S. Grain.
Major R.F.A.
D.T.M.O.
46th Divisional Artillery

Secret
CONFIDENTIAL.

--:--:--

WAR   DIARY

--:--:--

TRENCH MORTAR BATTERIES

--:--:--

FEBRUARY 1st: to FEBRUARY 28th: 1917.

****

WAR DIARY

Trench Mortar Batteries of 46th Divisional Artillery

INTELLIGENCE SUMMARY

Army Form C. 2118.

Place	Date	Hour	Summary of Events and Information	Remarks and references to Appendices
HEBUT.	Feb 1, 1917		Y.46 Battery fired 30 rounds and Z.46 Battery 102 rounds against enemy trenches in GOMMECOURT. One 2" mortar caused a secondary explosion in the enemy's lines, a large amount of white smoke being given off. Y.46 Battery registered new targets opposite MONCHY. Nothing to report.	
	2.		Y.46 Battery fired 12 rounds with great effect against enemy trenches in reply to hostile minenwerfer fire. X.46 Battery fired in counter offensive to enemy minenwerfers opposite same firing.	
	3.		N.46 Battery effectively replied to hostile minnies (M.C.) fire opposite GOMMECOURT.	
	4.		Nothing to report.	
	5.		9.45" mortars fired 29 rounds and 2" mortars 41 rounds against enemy trench system opposite MONCHY, badly damaging parts of the enemy front line trench.	
	6.		N.46 Battery fired 15 rounds registering enemy trenches opposite GOMMECOURT.	
	7.		Z.46 Battery fired 17 rounds in counter offensive to minenwerfer fire. The minenwerfers were silenced.	
	8.		3 a.m. was continued on 2" mortar emplacements opposite GOMMECOURT.	
	9.		N.46 and Y.46 Batteries replied to enemy mortar fire. Hostile mortars firing on the same principle as ours of which 6 mortars fired nine mine opposite MONCHY.	
	10.		X.46 and Z.46 fired nine mine opposite MONCHY damaging the considerably.	
	11.			
	12.			

WAR DIARY / INTELLIGENCE SUMMARY

Army Form C. 2118.

Trench Mortar Batteries or 46th Divisional Artillery

Place	Date	Hour	Summary of Events and Information	Remarks and references to Appendices
HENU	Feb 13. 1917		Nothing to report.	
	14.		T.M.B. opened fire at night 9 rounds in reply to enemy fire. The Battery fired 15 rounds against enemy trenches opposite GOMMECOURT and sprayed "D" Redoutte minenwerfer X/4 battery 8 rounds in enemy trenches to minenwerfer and 35 rounds against gun emplacements at MONCHY, Y/4 battery 21 rounds against enemy lines and Z/4 battery 24 rounds against minenwerfer and 80 rounds at enemy trenches at GOMMECOURT. T/4 shooting was good.	
	15.		T/4 battery fired 25 rounds at enemy wire opposite MONCHY, X/4 battery 105 rounds against the Chateau, GOMMECOURT, and Y/4 battery 2 series at enemy front and support lines. Y/4 battery observed accounting for 1/4 quantities of [?] and R.E. material. Y/4 battery fired 50 rounds and X + Y + Z 40 and 12 + 16 1 batteries 556 rounds at enemy trenches W. of GOMMECOURT claiming extensive damage to them. Y/4 battery also fired 10 rounds at enemy trenches N. of MONCHY's when a minenwerfer put the X/4 gunning team up. Three men were killed and one wounded.	
	16.		Nothing to report.	
	17.		T.M. Battery fired 6 rounds at an enemy battalion H.Q. admitted Gommecourt wood.	

WAR DIARY or INTELLIGENCE SUMMARY

Trench Mortar Battery 46th Divisional Artillery

Army Form C. 2118.

Place	Date	Hour	Summary of Events and Information	Remarks and references to Appendices
HENU	Feb. 1917 18 (contd)		X. t.6. Battery fired 140 rounds at enemy trenches opposite FONQUEVILLERS. It responded weakly.	
	19.		During the afternoon the enemy shelled 9/45 mortar position with 5.9" shells. Our fire effective. V.t.6. Battery fired 9 rounds at an enemy communication trench in reply to minenwerfer fire. This silenced the minenwerfer. Z.t.6. Battery registered two guns.	
	20.		V.t.6. Battery fired 14 rounds at an enemy trench mortar emplacement in reply to enemy fire. Two hostile minenwerfers stopped firing.	
	21.		3 rounds at spot.	
	22.		N.t.6. Battery fired in reply to one hostile mortar bomb. X.t.6. fired 11 rounds at enemy minenwerfer. Good effect.	
	23. & 24.		X.t.6. fired 70 rounds at enemy mine opposite MONCHY, rendering it passable. V.t. and N.t.6. Batteries both replied to minenwerfer fire.	
	24 & 25.		Z.t.6. Battery fired 88 rounds and V.t.6. Battery 8 rounds in organised reply to enemy shelling with Trench mortars at 9 O.M.E.COURT. X.t.6. Battery fired 26 rounds. Shooting was good for the same purpose.	
	26.		X.t.6. Battery fired 56 rounds at enemy trenches at MONCHY in reply to minenwerfer. Z.t.6. and V.t.6 Battery shot 10 rounds in registration.	

Army Form C. 2118.

WAR DIARY
Trench Mortar Batteries or Intelligence 46th Divisional Artillery
INTELLIGENCE SUMMARY
(Erase heading not required.)

Instructions regarding War Diaries and Intelligence Summaries are contained in F. S. Regs., Part II. and the Staff Manual respectively. Title Pages will be prepared in manuscript.

Place	Date	Hour	Summary of Events and Information	Remarks and references to Appendices
HENU	Feb 27 1917		In conjunction with 4.5" howitzers, 2/46 battery cut enemy's gaps in enemy wire N. of GOMMECOURT-FONQUEVILLERS road, and two passages gaps S. of the road. 286 rounds were fired. Y/46 battery fired with excellent effect at women against GOMMECOURT CHATEAU FARM and STABLES. X/46 battery and Y/46 battery fired incessantly at enemy minenwerfer fire at MONCHY. Nothing to report. C.B. dealt slightly with enemy by several but remained at duty.	
	28.			

M.E. Main
Capt. RFA
D.T.M.O.
46th Divisional Artillery

SECRET.

WAR DIARY.

TRENCH MORTAR BATTERIES.

MARCH 1st: to MARCh 31st: 1917.

WAR DIARY
INTELLIGENCE SUMMARY

Army Form C. 2118.

Trench Mortar Batteries 46th Divisional Artillery

Place	Date	Hour	Summary of Events and Information	Remarks and references to Appendices
HENU	MARCH			
	1.		On counter offensive to enemy Trench mortar fire X46 and Y46 Batteries fired 18 rounds at enemy Trenches opposite MONCHY.	nil
	2.		Y46 Battery fired 23 rounds with good effect at enemy Trenches opposite MONCHY.	nil
	3.		X46 Battery relieved Y46 Battery in action. X46 Battery replied to the enemy firing rifle grenades at our trenches. The enemy stopped firing at once.	nil
	4.		T46 and Y46 Batteries each placed one 2" mortar in action in PIGEON WOOD to fire on enemy posts in front of ESSARTS. Y46 Battery fired 9 rounds into the S. of MONCHY. The shooting was excellent.	nil
	5.		X46 Battery registered on enemy trenches at MONCHY. Y46 Battery placed a 9.45" mortar in action behind PIGEON WOOD.	nil
	6.		The 2" mortars in PIGEON WOOD fired 39 rounds against enemy posts. X46 and O.P.'s fired in action by enemy shell-fire. The Y46 and T46 Batteries fired 54 rounds against enemy strong points S. of ESSARTS. The mine in front of the points was badly damaged.	nil
	7.			nil
	8.		Y46 Battery fired 15 rounds and 2" mortar 32 rounds against enemy posts N. of PIGEON WOOD. The shooting was very effective.	nil
	9.		Y46 Battery relieved T46 Battery in action in PIGEON WOOD. Y46 Battery fired 15 rounds and Y46 Battery 66 rounds against enemy trenches S. of ESSARTS with good effect.	nil
	10.		X46 Battery fired 9 rounds at enemy trenches at MONCHY.	nil

WAR DIARY or INTELLIGENCE SUMMARY

Army Form C. 2118.

Trench Mortar Batteries — 46th Divisional Artillery

(Erase heading not required.)

Instructions regarding War Diaries and Intelligence Summaries are contained in F. S. Regs., Part II. and the Staff Manual respectively. Title Pages will be prepared in manuscript.

Place	Date MARCH	Hour	Summary of Events and Information	Remarks and references to Appendices
HENU	11.		X 46 Battery fired 10 rounds at enemy trenches at MONCHY.	
	12.		X 46 Battery fired 50 rounds at enemy front line with very good results, damaging the enemy trenches.	
	12-26		Trench Mortar provided men for road construction and carrying and salving ammunition in area captured from the enemy.	
	13.		Nothing to report.	
	14.		Y 46 Battery fired 10 rounds into MONCHY. Z 46 Battery placed a mortar in action to assist 139th Infantry Brigade firing 10 rounds. Batteries were employed in recovering advanced positions E. of GOMMECOURT.	
	15.		Three 9.45" mortars were handed over to 58th Division. Z 46 Battery fired 26 rounds against enemy loopholes.	
	16.		Nothing to report.	
	17.		One 9.45" mortar was handed over to 58th Division.	
	18.		One 9.45" mortar was handed over to 1.O.M. XVIII Corps.	
	19.		V 46, Y 46, T 46, Z 46 and W 46 Batteries moved from FONQUEVILLERS	
	20.		and GOMMECOURT to Billets in HENU. X 46 Battery moved from BIENVILLERS to HENU.	
	21.		Nothing to report.	
	22.		All Trench Mortar Batteries moved to Billets in FONQUEVILLERS	
	23-26		Batteries provided personnel for loading and sorting ammunition. All Batteries moved to Billets in HENU.	

WAR DIARY or INTELLIGENCE SUMMARY

Army Form C. 2118.

46 Divisional Artillery
Stencil marks Bats

Place	Date	Hour	Summary of Events and Information	Remarks and references to Appendices
	29		Marched to LE MAILLARD	
	30		Marched to BOUBERS	
	31		Marched to ANVIN	

R M Ovens
Capt RFA
a/ DAMO 46a D.A.

Army Form C. 2118.

WAR DIARY
or
INTELLIGENCE SUMMARY
(Erase heading not required.)

Instructions regarding War Diaries and Intelligence Summaries are contained in F. S. Regs., Part II. and the Staff Manual respectively. Title Pages will be prepared in manuscript.

Place	Date	Hour	Summary of Events and Information	Remarks and references to Appendices
	1/3/17		Marched from Louvencourt to Vadencourt.	
	2/3/17		Marched from Vadencourt to Senlis through Fowler, Val de Maricourt.	
	3/3/17		Returned 158th T.M. Bay at Beaucourt.	
	4/3/17 & 5/3/17		In the line at Beaucourt. Rec'd were relieved by 10th K.O.Y.L.I.'s on 5th and went back to Senlis.	
	6/3/17		Relay at Louvencourt.	
	7/3/17		Marched to Bagneux.	
	8/3/17 & 9/3/17		Rested at Bagneux.	
	10/3/17		Marched from Bagneux to Senlis through another valley at Vadencourt.	
	11/3/17		Marched from Senlis to Hebuterne through Bouzincourt.	
	12/3/17		Marched from Hebuterne Bivouac to Bivouac through Puisieux Bivouac and Sheni.	
	13/3/17		Marched from Sheni to Bacourt through Len.	
	20/3/17		Returned at Bacourt.	
	21/3/17		Detrained at Erquinghem and marched to Fleurbaix through Sailly through Romarin and St Yvon.	
	22/3/17 to 31/3/17		In the line.	

J.F. Rafferty
C 157 T.M. Bay

CONFIDENTIAL.

WAR DIARY.

TRENCH MORTAR BATTERIES.

APRIL 1st: to APRIL 30th: 1917.

WAR DIARY or INTELLIGENCE SUMMARY

Div TRENCH MORTAR BATTERIES

Army Form C. 2118.

(Erase heading not required.)

Place	Date	Hour	Summary of Events and Information	Remarks and references to Appendices
L'ANVIN	Apr 1st		Marched to Billets at MAZINGHAM.	
MAZINGHAM	2/4/17 to 12/4/17		Carried out scheme of training. Physical drill daily. Route marches in full marching order, 3 times weekly. 2" Trench Mortars Gun drill. Rifle and Machine Drill. Particular attention was paid to training in visual signalling and anti-gas drill.	
MAZINGHAM	6/4/17		Special parade for presentation of medals. The following O.R's in Trench Mortars were presented with Military Medals:- 820087. Bomb. Toillon E.H. V/46 Heavy Trench Mortar Battery for the following act of bravery :- On 14th Feb. 1917. Bomb. Toillon was a member of a detachment firing a 9.45" Trench Mortar. One round was a misfire and Bomb. Toillon returned at once to the gun pit. He found the fuze of the bomb was burning. Bomb. Toillon at once unscrewed the fuze which was a 31.6. per to burn for 21 seconds and knew it away slightly scorching his hand in the operation. It was entirely due to the prompt action of this N.C.O in unscrewing the fuze that the bomb did not explode in the mortar. On unloading the bomb it was found that the primer of the propellant had burned, but not the propellant itself, this continued	

46 DIV TRENCH MORTAR BATTERIES

WAR DIARY or INTELLIGENCE SUMMARY

Army Form C. 2118.

Place	Date	Hour	Summary of Events and Information	Remarks and references to Appendices
MAZINGHAM	6/4/17		apparently being not sufficient to force the bomb out of the gun, but sufficient to arm the fuze. Two of the mortar detachment, in addition to Bdr. Heillon, saw the fuze burning. 82021 S Gnr. Rane J. Y/46 T.M.B. for the following act of bravery:- On Apr. 16th 1916, on opening fire on enemy front line trenches, in reply to an enemy trench mortar, the mortar which he was helping to serve was vigorously shelled by the enemy mortar. He assisted to man the mortar, and fire on the hostile mortar, ultimately forcing it to withdraw. Again, on Apr. 19th, he kept to his gun under heavy shell fire.	
MAZINGHAM	9/4/17		Marched with the Division on a Divisional Route March, in Field Service Marching Order. Route:- MAZINGHAM, AUCHY-AU-BOIS, ESTREE-BLANCHE, MAZINGHAM. Inspected by Corps Commander en route.	
L'ECLEME	13/4/17		Marched to L'ECLEME.	
do.	14/4/17 to 22/4/17		Carried out Scheme of training. Physical drill daily. Route marches in full Marching order, three times weekly. 2" Trench Mortar Gun drill Rifle and Marching. Lectures, Anti gas drill. Special attention paid to visual signalling, and field training in Map reading.	

WAR DIARY
or
INTELLIGENCE SUMMARY
(Erase heading not required.)

46 Dn TRENCH Army FOR(C) 2118. BATTERIES

Place	Date	Hour	Summary of Events and Information	Remarks and references to Appendices
L'ECLEME	22/4/17		Battery Commanders proceeded to GRENAY to carry out a reconnaissance of the front to be taken over from the 24th Division.	
BULLY GRENAY.	23/4/17		Marched into Billets in BULLY GRENAY.	
do.	24/4/17		Took over from D.T.M.O. 24th Division. one 9.45" and four 2" trench mortars taken over from 24th Division in action and four 2" trench mortars handed over to 24th Division in exchange.	
BULLY GRENAY.	25/4/17. 26/4/17. 30/4/17.		Several reconnaissances of front by OC's selecting positions.	
do.	27/4/17		Guns withdrawn from existing positions and commenced preparing more suitable ones.	
do.	28/4/17		Z/46 T.M. Bty. put 2 guns in action about M.30.a.3.9 (Ref:- Map. France Sheet 36.C.SW. 1/20.000.)	
do.	29/4/17		Y/46 (Heavy) Trench Mortar Battery put in bed for trench mortar at M.23.d 65.95. (Ref:- Map. Sheet. 36.C.SW. 1/20.000). Took over Heavy Trench Mortars from 6th Division. Z/46 Trench Bty fired 43 rds. to support an Infantry raid. Target:- Enemy T.M.s in M.24.B. Y/46 (Heavy) Trench Mortar Battery mounted 1 gun. Ammunition carried to position. also to 2" positions.	

(continued).

46 DIV TRENCH MORTAR BATTERIES.

WAR DIARY
or
INTELLIGENCE SUMMARY.

Army Form C. 2118.

(Erase heading not required.)

Place	Date	Hour	Summary of Events and Information	Remarks and references to Appendices
BULLY GRENAY	30/4/17		2 ORs wounded (V Battery). 4 positions prepared for X Battery at N.7.a. 3.5.	

M Mond
Captain R.F.A.
A.D.T.M.O. 46th Divisional Artillery

CONFIDENTIAL.

WAR DIARY.

TRENCH MORTAR BATTERIES.

MAY 1st: to MAY 31st: 1917.

Army Form C. 2118.

WAR DIARY
or
INTELLIGENCE SUMMARY.
(Erase heading not required.)

46th Divisional Trench Mortars

Instructions regarding War Diaries and Intelligence Summaries are contained in F.S. Regs., Part II. and the Staff Manual respectively. Title pages will be prepared in manuscript.

Place	Date	Hour	Summary of Events and Information	Remarks and references to Appendices
BULLY GRENAY	1/5/17		2/Lieut. E.J. Graham took command of Z/46 Trench Mortar Battery. Posted from 231 Brigade R.F.A.	
"	2/5/17		Took over gun from 61 Division (Heavy). Moving up tonight two medium mortars with ammunition.	
"	3/5/17		2 OR's y & bh" wounded - remained at duty Z/46 T.M. Battery fired 19 rounds on enemy M.G's in M. 24. b.	
"	4/5/17		2 OR's y & bh" wounded. Z/46 Trench Mortar Battery fired 20 rounds on enemy Trench Mortar emplacements in M 24. b.1. with excellent effect. One round caused a dense mass of white smoke. X/46 Trench Mortar Battery fired 5 rounds during night in retaliation for enemy Trench Mortars which were silenced.	
"	5/5/17		Z/46 Trench Mortar Battery fired 8 rounds in retaliation for enemy Trench Mortars which were silenced just before dawn. In the afternoon Z Battery fired 17 rounds on enemy Trench Mortar emplacements, with good results. V/46 Heavy Trench Mortar Battery fired 20 rounds on enemy	

Army Form C. 2118.

46th Divisional Trench Mortars

WAR DIARY
or
INTELLIGENCE SUMMARY.
(Erase heading not required.)

Place	Date	Hour	Summary of Events and Information	Remarks and references to Appendices
BULLY GRENAY	5/5/17		Trench Mortar emplacement and trenches doing great damage. 2" Trench Mortars fired 20 rounds on row of houses about M.24.d.5.4 on 4th inst with good results.	
"	6/5/17		Capt G.G. Lowndes wounded and evacuated. V/46 Trench Mortar Battery fired 20 rounds on Hill 65 doing damage to houses.	
"	5/5/17		X/46 Trench Mortar Battery fired 5 rounds in retaliation to enemy Trench Mortars about 11.0 p.m.) and silenced them. Bright moonlight night made observation possible. A house about N.7.6. 02.42 was observed to be demolished. Z/46 Trench Mortar Battery fired 8 rounds in retaliation to enemy Trench Mortars in M.24.b. silencing them. Also 17 rounds on afternoon of 5th on enemy Trench Mortar emplacements in M.24.d. with good effect. During the night 5th/6th May Z/46 Trench Mortar Battery fired 45 rounds on Hill 65 and X/46 Trench Mortar Battery 10 rounds on to the railway in N.13.	
"	7/5/17		Lieut N. Gitten took command of V/46 Trench Mortar Battery and Capt. L.R. Mawas took over the duties of D.T.M.O. V/46 Trench Mortar Battery fired 20 rounds on M.24.d 35.15 with good effect and X/46 and Z/46 Trench Mortar Batteries fired in counter offensive at request of Infantry.	

Army Form C. 2118.

WAR DIARY
or
INTELLIGENCE SUMMARY. 46th Divisional Trench Mortar Batteries

(Erase heading not required.)

Place	Date	Hour	Summary of Events and Information	Remarks and references to Appendices
BULLY GRENAY.	8/5/17.		Lieut. L. Balme joined from 46th D.T.C. and took command of X/46 Trench Mortar Battery. V/46 Trench Mortar Battery fired 20 rounds at Hill 65 demolishing a house. X/46 and Z/46 Trench Mortar Batteries fired on enemy Trench Mortars and enemy trenches.	
"	9/5/17.		V/46 Heavy Trench Mortar Battery fired on the enemy in the open who were round one of our aeroplanes which had been shot down, and dispersed them. Y/46 Trench Mortar Battery fired 13 rounds about N.7.b.00.50 in retaliation at request of the Infantry. Bombs were observed to fall in the enemy trenches.	
"	10/5/17.		V/46 Heavy Trench Mortar Battery fired 30 rounds at T.M. and M.G. emplacement. Z/46 Trench Mortar Battery fired 27 rounds on trenches and enemy T.M. positions with good effect.	
"	11/5/17.		V/46 Heavy Trench Mortar Battery continued to fire at Hill 65. Z/46 Trench Mortar Battery fired 48 rounds on enemy trenches.	
"	12/5/17.		V/46 Heavy Trench Mortar Battery fired 20 & Z/46 Trench Mortar Battery fired 66 rounds at Hill 65 & trenches. No.1 gun of V/46 Heavy Trench taken up to position on night 12th/13th.	

Army Form C. 2118.

WAR DIARY
or
INTELLIGENCE SUMMARY. 46th Divisional Trench Mortars
(Erase heading not required.)

Place	Date	Hour	Summary of Events and Information	Remarks and references to Appendices
Bully Grenay	13/5/17		The ground under No.2 bed gave way and the gun has been taken out to make a new bed. Casualties - 1 N.C.O killed + 1 Gunner killed (Z/46 TMB).	
"	14/5/17		Work on the alternative positions continued. Nothing in firing to report.	
"	15/5/17		Y/46 Heavy Trench Mortar Battery moved No.4 gun to new position and No.1 gun was brought into action. 20 rounds fired by Z/46 Trench Mortar Battery at suspected M.G. emplacement at M.24.d.30.20, several "hits" being obtained.	
"	16/5/17		Considerable damage was done to trenches about M.24.d.70.20 by Heavy Trench Mortar Battery & direct hits obtained on Lewis about M.24.d.30.10 by Medium Battery.	
"	17/5/17		10 rounds fired at NASH ALLEY by Y/46 Heavy Trench Mortar Battery - 5 direct hits being obtained in the trench. X/46 Trench Mortar Battery fired at enemy T.M. positions at No.7.G.10.70 with good effect. Trench Mortar Batteries carried out cooperation on 17th in support of raid by 139th Inf Bde on night 17/18th. Y/46 Heavy Trench Mortar Battery with one round blew up an enemy	
"	18/5/17		bomb store in NASH ALLEY. X/46 Trench Mortar Battery fired 60 rounds in support of our Infantry Operation. After first few rounds enemy ceased to send up Very lights in this sector. Y/46 Trench Mortar Battery cut wire in front of NASH ALLEY doing damage to the wire. The gun positions and	

WAR DIARY
or
INTELLIGENCE SUMMARY. 46th Divisional Trench Mortars

Army Form C. 2118.

(Erase heading not required.)

Place	Date	Hour	Summary of Events and Information	Remarks and references to Appendices
Bully Grenay	18/5/17 contd		O.P. were kept under shrapnel fire during firing and the O.P. had to be left. The positions were also fired on by enemy rifle grenades. Z/46 Trench Mortar Battery cut wire in front of AHEAD Trench successfully. Casualties :- 1 O.R. (Y/46 TMB) Killed and 1 OR (Y/46 TMB) wounded, caused by a premature which put both guns out of action.	2 Medium Mortars taken over from 1st Army T.M. School.
"	19/5/17		DYNAMITE MAGAZINE in N.1.d. and also M.G. emplacement at N.1.d.18.79. were fired on with good result by Y/46 Heavy Trench Mortar Battery. Visibility was bad during this period. Enemy front line in front of CITE ST LAURENT was fired on by X/46 Trench Mortar Battery, but observation as to amount of damage done was impossible owing to the light. One gun of Z/46 Trench Mortar Battery out of action.	
"	20/5/17		Trench at N.1. b. 20. 54 was demolished by the Heavy Battery and also the reservoir on Hill 65. N.25.a. was fired at by same battery destroying part of the buildings. Y/46 Heavy Trench Mortar Battery fired into FOSSE 3 (M.30.6.) doing great damage to sheds, Boiler House, & other buildings. This was running for 3 hours. During firing of Z/46 Trench Mortar Battery on AHEAD TRENCH, one round caused an explosion, probably an enemy bomb store. Casualties :- 1 OR. (V/46 H.TM B) Killed.	Wire cutting in front of NASHALLEY was carried out on 19th, 20th & 21st preliminary to an attack on 21/5/17
"	21/5/17			

Army Form C. 2118.

WAR DIARY
or
INTELLIGENCE SUMMARY. 46th Divisional Trench Mortars

(Erase heading not required.)

Place	Date	Hour	Summary of Events and Information	Remarks and references to Appendices
Bully Grenay	22/5/17		V/46 Heavy Trench Mortar Battery did great damage to Mine Buildings in FOSSE 3. Enemy retaliated on position with 4·2's How. and Light Minenwerfers. A medium Minenwerfer battery was observed firing at M.30.d.77.68, and was immediately silenced by the Heavy Battery in accordance with O.O.92. X & Y/46 Trench Mortar Batteries cut wire in front of NASH ALLEY. Z/46 Trench Mortar Battery cut wire in front of AHEAD TRENCH with good effect and fired in retaliation to enemy T.M's during the night 22/23rd.	
"	23/5/17		V/46 Heavy Trench Mortar Battery fired on FOSSE 3, doing damage to "Steelwork" and Buildings in the FOSSE & Several direct "hits" on the trench. X & Y/46 Trench Mortar Batteries again cut wire in front of NASH ALLEY, which was destroyed in many places. The enemy has been filling up the gaps with concertina wire. Z/46 Trench Mortar Battery fired in retaliation to enemy T.M's during the night 23rd/24th.	
"	24/5/17		In support of an attack by 137th Infantry Brigade to capture and hold NASH ALLEY and NETLEY TRENCH Medium trench mortars bombarded the DYNAMITE MAGAZINE & the junction of NASH and NESTOR TRENCHES. V/46 Trench Mortar Battery fired into FOSSE 3 in M.30.b. & ALMANAC TRENCH with good effect. Also wire cutting was again carried out in front of NASH ALLEY. (continued)	

Army Form C. 2118.

WAR DIARY
or
INTELLIGENCE SUMMARY. 46th Divisional Trench Mortars
(Erase heading not required.)

Place	Date	Hour	Summary of Events and Information	Remarks and references to Appendices
Bully Grenay	24/5/17		From 12 noon 24th to 7pm 24th X & Y Trench Mortar Batteries fired 95 rounds in cutting wire in front of NASH ALLEY with very good effect clearing all the wire that could be seen. The Infantry Brigadier and Colonel in the line reported that all the wire had been successfully cut and cleared away. From 7pm 33 rounds were fired by same batteries into DYNAMITE MAGAZINE. and at NIA. 25. 55.	
"	25/5/17		Z/46 Trench Mortar Battery fired 48 rounds in retaliation to hostile T.M's into houses and AHEAD and ALCOVE TRENCHES during the night 24th/25th.	
"	26/5/17		V/46 Heavy Trench Mortar Battery fired on houses in M.24.d. Two cellars were apparently blown up.	
"	27/5/17		Carrying parties have failed during the last few days in getting ammunition up to the guns which accounts for the few rounds fired. V/46 Heavy Trench Mortar Battery fired on an enemy T.M. emplacement doing considerable damage. In retaliation to enemy T.M's in the early morning Z/46 Trench Mortar Battery fired with good effect into AHEAD TRENCH.	
"	28/5/17		Nothing to report.	

WAR DIARY
or
INTELLIGENCE SUMMARY. 46th Divisional Trench Mortars

Army Form C. 2118.

Place	Date	Hour	Summary of Events and Information	Remarks and references to Appendices
Bully Grenay	29/5/17		Casualties:- Lieut. A.S. Lee wounded and admitted to Hospital and 1 O.R. killed and 1 O.R. wounded but remained at duty. (all Z/46 Tr.M.Battery).	
	29/5/17		O.O. No. 94 issued to O.C. V, Y & Z Batteries as preliminary orders. These batteries believe this date and the morning of 2/6/17 are to conduct positions & the guns to be ready for action. They will cut wire in front of AHEAD TRENCH. Date and times of this operation to be notified later.	
			V/46 Heavy Trench Mortar Battery fired on to "Hill 65" doing considerable damage to trenches. In the early morning Z/46 Trench Mortar Battery retaliated with good effect on to AHEAD TRENCH to hostile T.Ms.	
	30/5/17		First Army Summary 867 reports under information from Enemy Prisoners that one Company of 153rd. Regt. suffered 15 casualties from our Trench Mortars. This apparently refers to firing of X and Y/46 Trench Mortar Batteries who were firing at NASH ALLEY on that day.	
	29/5/17		2/Lieut L.S. Martin (S.R.) joined for attachment to Y/46 Trench Mortar Battery from England.	
	30/5/17		In retaliation to hostile T.Ms during the afternoon Z/46 Trench Mortar Battery fired on AHEAD TRENCH, and Lewis at N.30. B. 30. 35. Enemy report M.G. at this house was silenced.	

Army Form C. 2118.

WAR DIARY
or
INTELLIGENCE SUMMARY. 46th Divisional Trench Mortars
(Erase heading not required.)

Place	Date	Hour	Summary of Events and Information	Remarks and references to Appendices
BULLY GRENAY.	31/5/17		Owing to reliefs taking place by the Infantry, the Battalion Commander requested V/46 Heavy Trench Mortar Battery not to fire. X/46 Trench Mortar Battery cut wire in front of NASH ALLEY with good effect, Also an entrance to a dug out blown in as several pieces of timber was blown up out of the trench Casualties :- 2 O.Rs (X/46 T.M. Bty.) wounded by a premature from our own mortar.	

QRMurray
Captain R.F.A.
A.D.T.M.O. 46th Div. Artillery.

CONFIDENTIAL.

WAR DIARY.

TRENCH MORTAR BATTERIES.

JUNE 1st: to JUNE 30th: 1917.

Army Form C. 2118.

WAR DIARY
or
INTELLIGENCE SUMMARY. 46th Division Heavy & Medium Trench Mortar Batteries.

(Erase heading not required.)

Instructions regarding War Diaries and Intelligence Summaries are contained in F. S. Regs., Part II. and the Staff Manual respectively. Title pages will be prepared in manuscript.

Place	Date	Hour	Summary of Events and Information	Remarks and references to Appendices
Bully Grenay	1/6/17	00.10	95 issued ordering the relief in action of Z/46 Medium Trench Mortar Battery by Y/46 Trench Mortar Battery on 3/6/17. Y/46 Heavy Trench Mortar Battery was requested by the Infantry not to fire owing to relief. Z/46 Trench Mortar Battery fired during the night in counter offensive to hostile Trench Mortars.	
do.	2/6/17.		Y/46 Heavy Trench Mortar Battery fired at trenches and ruins on Hill 65 about M.24.d. 50.40 doing considerable damage to trenches and ruins. Z/46 Trench Mortar Battery fired 47 rounds in counter offensive to hostile Trench Mortars. Hostile Trench Mortars ceased firing and enemy retaliated on our T.M. position with 5.9 How's: (Casualties 1 O.R. V/46 T.M.By wounded.)	
do.	3/6/17		Y/46 Heavy Trench Mortar Battery fired on ABODE TRENCH and ruins on Hill 65 doing considerable damage to trench and ruins, bricks and timber being thrown up. Z/46 Trench Mortar Battery fired on ALCOVE and AHEAD Trenches in retaliation to hostile T.M's. Considerable damage was done to	

2353 Wt. W2544/1454 700,000 5/15 D. D. & L. A.D.S.S./Forms/C. 2118.

Army Form C. 2118.

WAR DIARY
or
INTELLIGENCE SUMMARY

(Erase heading not required.)

46th Div. Heavy and Medium T.M. Batteries.

Place	Date	Hour	Summary of Events and Information	Remarks and references to Appendices
Bully Grenay	3/6/17 4/6/17		ALCOVE Trench, earth and timber being thrown up. Z/46 Trench Mortar Battery was relieved in action by Y/46 Trench Mortar Battery. X/46 Trench Mortar Battery fired 24 rounds on to wire in front of NASH ALLEY (N.1.a.80.70 r.c.). 15 rounds were observed to fall on wire with good effect. Y/46 Trench Mortar Battery fired on houses in M.24.b. in counter offensive to hostile Trench Mortar. Casualties:- 2/Lieut G.P.Clay (Y/46 T.M.Bty.) wounded but remained at duty.	
"	5/6/17		V/46 Heavy Trench Mortar Battery fired at the RESERVOIR in N.25.a., several direct hits being obtained, doing considerable damage to ruins. 90 rounds fired on wire and in NASH ALLEY, effect by X/46 Trench Mortar Battery. During the night, Y/46 Trench Mortar Battery fired in counter offensive to hostile Trench Mortars, and also fired 29 rounds in wire cutting in accordance with Operation Orders received.	
"	6/6/17		V/46 Heavy Trench Mortar Battery fired into FOSSE 3 (M.30.b.). Iron girders & sheets of iron were thrown into the air. A great	

Army Form C. 2118.

WAR DIARY
or
INTELLIGENCE SUMMARY.
46 Div. Heavy and Medium T.M. Batteries.

(Erase heading not required.)

Instructions regarding War Diaries and Intelligence Summaries are contained in F.S. Regs., Part II. and the Staff Manual respectively. Title pages will be prepared in manuscript.

Place	Date	Hour	Summary of Events and Information	Remarks and references to Appendices
Bully Grenay	6/6/17		amount of damage was done to the buildings. Feeble retaliation on the part of the enemy. X/46 Trench Mortar Battery fired on wire in front of NASH ALLEY at N.1.a. 80.75. The wire was observed to be blown up and scattered. Y/46 Trench Mortar Battery fired during the night 576K on HOUSES, HILL 65 in counter offensive to hostile trench mortars. V/46 Heavy Trench Mortar Battery silenced a Medium Minenwerfer Battery observed firing from M.24.d. 90.68. Z/46 Trench Mortar Battery moved up into action and fired 60 rounds on wire from M.30.a. 95.95 to M.30.b. 06.57. with good results. X/46 Trench Mortar Battery cut wire in front of NASH ALLEY with good results.	
"	7/6/17		2/Lieut J.H. Waddingham joined Trench Mortar Batteries from Base, and was posted to command Z/46 Trench Mortar Battery. 2 guns of V/46 Heavy Trench Mortar Battery and 8 guns of Y & Z Batteries demolished buildings, machine gun and trench mortar emplacements, trenches and cut wire about HILL 65 from 5am to	
"	8/6/17			

Army Form C. 2118.

WAR DIARY
or
INTELLIGENCE SUMMARY.
46th Div. Heavy and Medium T.M. Batteries.

(Erase heading not required.)

Place	Date	Hour	Summary of Events and Information	Remarks and references to Appendices
Bully Grenay	8/6/17	8.30 p.m.	V/46 Heavy Trench Mortar Battery fired 220 rounds and the Xree Medium Trench Mortars fired 939 rounds during the 7th and 8th. V/46 Heavy Trench Mortar Battery did very considerable damage to targets allotted to them and as far as is known created a record by firing 130 rounds in fifteen hours from one Heavy Trench Mortar. Y and Z/46 Trench Mortar Batteries completely cut and cleared away all the wire that could be seen and from reports received from the Infantry completely cut all wire that was allotted to them. The detachments although under fire from hostile trench mortars, 4.2's and 77 m.m's (many direct "Hits" being obtained on the emplacements) most of the time, worked extremely well. Casualties :- 4 ORs (Z/46 T.M. Bty) wounded and admitted to hospital, 2 ORs (X/46 T.M. Bty) wounded and admitted to hospital. X/46 Trench Mortar Battery fired on wire in front of NASH ALLEY. Z/46 Trench Mortar Battery had two positions destroyed	

Army Form C. 2118.

WAR DIARY
or
INTELLIGENCE SUMMARY.   46th Div Heavy and Medium J. M. Batteries

(Erase heading not required.)

Instructions regarding War Diaries and Intelligence Summaries are contained in F. S. Regs., Part II. and the Staff Manual respectively. Title pages will be prepared in manuscript.

Place	Date	Hour	Summary of Events and Information	Remarks and references to Appendices
Bully Grenay	8/6/17		by shell fire, but one gun being undamaged was brought into action again.	
do.	9/6/17		Nothing to report. - No firing.	
do.	10/6/17		Y/46 Trench Mortar Battery bombarded trench from M.30.b.12.50 to M.30.b.10.25.	
do.	11/6/17		Lieut G.J. Graham Z/46 Trench Mortar Battery returned to 231st Brigade R.F.A. 2/Lieut J H Waddingham joined from BAC and took over command.	
do.	12/6/17		Operation Order No. 97 issued to X Battery's giving instructions and "targets" and wire to be cut in conjunction with 137th Infantry Brigade raiding the German Front Line between N.1.d. 16.16 and N.7.a. 97.50. X/46 Trench Mortar Battery carried out wire cutting operations and took on "targets" as detailed in the Operation Order. 10R (V/46 TMBty) awarded "Medaille Militaire" by Army Commander	
do	13/6/17			
do.	14/6/17		Y/46 Heavy Trench Mortar Battery fired 33 rounds into AB50.OM TRENCH between M.24.b.70.10 and M.24.b.70.30. doing considerable damage to trench and trench mortar emplacement at M.24.d. 75.45; 3 direct	

WAR DIARY

INTELLIGENCE SUMMARY. 46th Div Heavy

7 Aeroplanes 7. T.O. Blair

Army Form C. 2118.

Place	Date	Hour	Summary of Events and Information	Remarks and references to Appendices
Bully Grenay	14/6/17		Nils: being obtained and throwing up a large amount of timber etc. X/46 Trench Mortar Battery carried out wire cutting. Y/46 Trench Mortar Battery fired during the night in counter operations to hostile trench Mortars. Lieut F. Chapman (Y/46 T.M.Bty.) admitted to Hospital	
do.	15/6/17		Operation order 98/1 issued ordering the relief by X/46 Trench Mortar Battery in action by Z/46 Trench Mortar Battery. O.C. Z/46 Trench Mortar Battery reconnoitred the line to be covered and relief was completed by 7.30 p.m. Hostile Trench Mortar firing from M.24.d.88.79 (about) was silenced twice during the night by V/46 Heavy Trench Mortar Battery. Y/46 Trench Mortar Battery fired in counter operations to hostile trench mortars during the night with good effect.	
do.	16/6/17		Y/46 Trench Mortar Battery fired 18 rounds at 3-0 and 3-30 p.m. in counter operations to hostile trench Mortars. V/46 Heavy Trench Mortar Battery fired 14 rounds at trench Mortar emplacement about M.24.d.88.79 and silenced enemy trench Mortars.	

WAR DIARY or INTELLIGENCE SUMMARY

Army Form C. 2118.

4th Div. Heavy and Medium T.M. Btties.

Place	Date	Hour	Summary of Events and Information	Remarks and references to Appendices
Bully Grenay	16/6/17		Operation Order No. 99 issued to Y/46 Trench Mortar Battery ordering the bombardment same day of L shaped house and trench running in front from M.30.b.15.50 to M.30.b.15.25 with as many guns as can	
		5.6" 6 p.m.	be brought to bear on this target in conjunction with the Corps Heavy Artillery. 62 rounds were fired by Y/46 Trench Mortar Battery at this target with very good effect.	
do.	17/6/17		V/46 Heavy Trench Mortar Battery silenced a hostile trench Mortar firing from M.24.d.88.79.	
do.	18/6/17		Y/46 Trench Mortar Battery fired during the morning in counter offensive to hostile trench mortars. V/46 Heavy Trench Mortar Battery silenced a hostile trench Mortar firing from M.24.d.90.75. At request of Infantry Y/46 Trench Mortar Battery cut wire in front of L shaped house.	
do.	19/6/17		V/46 Heavy & Y/46 Medium Trench Mortar Batteries fired on to Hill 65 during the night 19th/20th to assist in preventing counter attacks. One Heavy Mortar being put out of action by	

Army Form C. 2118.

WAR DIARY
or
INTELLIGENCE SUMMARY. 46th Div. Heavy and Medium T.M. Btes.

(Erase heading not required.)

Place	Date	Hour	Summary of Events and Information	Remarks and references to Appendices
Bully Grenay	19/6/17.		Shell fire, and three 2 inch positions were blown in.	
do.	20/6/17.		V/46 Heavy and Y/46 Medium Trench Mortar Batteries fired in counter offensive to hostile trench mortars. Z/46 Trench Mortar Battery out wire in front of CITE ST EDOUARD. Operation Order No 100 issued ordering the relief in action of Y/46 Trench Mortar Battery by X/46 Trench Mortar Battery on 21st. at RIAUMONT.	
		4·0a.m.	V/46 Heavy Trench Mortar Battery fired 20 rounds between 1·45 and 4·0a.m. on to HILL 65 to prevent enemy massing in AHEAD TRENCH.	
			Y/46 Trench Mortar Battery fired 18 rounds into AHEAD TRENCH between 1·0 and 3·30a.m. One heavy trench mortar belonging to Y/46 Heavy Trench Mortar Battery put out of action by a direct hit on the platform. Three 2 inch positions and a bomb store blown in and mortars undamaged.	
do.	21/6/17		V/46 Heavy Trench Mortar fired during the night sub. AHEAD TRENCH about M.24d. 40.30 to harass the enemy, and Y/46 Trench Mortar Battery fired on to HILL 65 in counter offensive to hostile trench mortars.	

Army Form C. 2118.

WAR DIARY
or
INTELLIGENCE SUMMARY

46th Div. Heavy and Medium T.M. Batteries.

(Erase heading not required.)

Instructions regarding War Diaries and Intelligence Summaries are contained in F.S. Regs., Part II. and the Staff Manual respectively. Title pages will be prepared in manuscript.

Place	Date	Hour	Summary of Events and Information	Remarks and references to Appendices
Bully Grenay	21/6/17	5pm to 3am	40 rounds were fired by 2/46 Trench Mortar Battery into enemy front line about N.7.a.90.60 with very good effect. No.820.466 Corpl. Watson A.H. (V/46 Trench Mortar Battery) and No. 820.686 Gnr. Vixon G. (V/46 Heavy Trench Mortar Battery) received the Military Medal Ribbons by Lieut. General A.E.A. Holland, C.B. M.V.O. D.S.O. V/46 Heavy Trench Mortar Battery worked on two new positions and ammunition carrying. X and V/46 Trench Mortar positions which had been destroyed by Batteries worked on positions X and Y/46 Trench Mortar Battery cut a good gap 20 yards wide in enemy wire at N.7.a. 90.50.00 to N.7.a.101 issued 16 x 4hr ordering wire cutting on 22/6/17. V/46 Heavy Trench Mortar Battery fired during the afternoon in counter offensive to hostile trench mortars. X/46 Trench Mortar	
do.	22/6/17			
do.	22/6/17		Battery worked on preparing positions in readiness for an attack on 28th. by 137th Infantry Brigade. Z/46 Trench Mortar Battery did no firing owing to two emplacements being destroyed and guns put out of action. 2 new mortars were sent up and	

WAR DIARY or INTELLIGENCE SUMMARY

Army Form C. 2118.

46th Div. Heavy and Medium T.M. Batteries.

Place	Date	Hour	Summary of Events and Information	Remarks and references to Appendices
Bully Grenay.	23/6/17 and 24/6/17.		were ready for action same night. Casualties:- 1 O.R. (v.Bty) wounded. Operation Order No. 102 issued to A, V, X, Y Trench Mortar Batteries with reference to an attack by 137th Infantry Brigade on 24/6/17, on AHEAD and ADMIRAL trenches. 2 inch trench mortars to cut wire in front of AHEAD TRENCH from ALICE to M.24.d.22.20.	
	25/6/17.		9.45 inch trench mortars to bombard AGNES East of M.24.d.40.30. 15 rounds fired by V/46 Heavy Trench Mortar Battery at M.24.d.68.40 doing considerable damage. In support of operations by 137th Infantry Brigade, 40 rounds were fired into AGNES TRENCH between M.24.d.70.42 and M.24.d.40.32 with very good effect, one round apparently fell in a cellar or dug out blowing up a large quantity of timber and bricks. No. 3 Gun of same battery now in action and ammunition carried up. Work being carried on at M18.c.89.55. (No. 4 position) at M18.d.00.64. (No. 4 position). X/46 Trench Mortar Battery fired 120 rounds in cutting wire in front of AHEAD TRENCH between ALICE and M.24.d.22.20 with very	

Army Form C. 2118.

WAR DIARY
or
INTELLIGENCE SUMMARY.
46th Div. Heavy and Medium T.M. Batteries
(Erase heading not required.)

Instructions regarding War Diaries and Intelligence Summaries are contained in F.S. Regs., Part II. and the Staff Manual respectively. Title pages will be prepared in manuscript.

Place	Date	Hour	Summary of Events and Information	Remarks and references to Appendices
Bully Grenay	25/6/17		good effect, wire being cut in many places. 80 rounds were fired on enemy front line at M.7.a. 90.50 and houses about M.7.b. at 12.45 a.m. by Z/46 Casualties ;- 2 OR's killed & 1 OR wounded (Z/46 T.M.Bty). X/46 Trench Mortar Battery advanced two mortars during the evening to position at M.24.c. 87.20.	
"	26/5/17		Y/46 Heavy Trench Mortar Battery placed No. 4 gun in position at M.18.c. 89.55 but owing to no call from Infantry being received no firing was done. X/46 Trench Mortar Battery placed 4 mortars in forward position in Railway cutting. Infantry were informed of this, but were not called on to fire. No. 820368 Gnr. PROCTOR F.G. (Y/46 T.M. Bty) presented with Military Medal ribbon by Divisional Commander, Major-General W. Thwaites, C.B.	
"	27/6/17		Operation Order No. 103 issued ordering the relief of Z/46 Trench Mortar Battery in action by Y/46 Trench Mortar Battery on the 29/6/19. X/46 Trench Mortar Battery carried ammunition to new position. Infantry at request of Infantry, 10 rounds were not called on to fire.	

WAR DIARY
or
INTELLIGENCE SUMMARY.

Army Form C. 2118.

46th Div. Heavy and Medium T.M. Batteries.

Place	Date	Hour	Summary of Events and Information	Remarks and references to Appendices
Bully Grenay	27/6/17.		were fired on enemy front line at N.7.a.90.60. Operation Order No.96 received from 46th Divisional Artillery, giving "targets" for Heavy Trench mortars in support of an attack on 28/6/17 by 137, 138 + 139 Infantry Brigades.	
	28/6/17.		Y/46 Heavy Trench Mortar Battery fired 28 rounds between 4/mm and 6/mm on to houses about N.19.a.10.40., N.19.c.60.60., and N.19.c.70.95. in support of the above attack. Also 13 rounds fired at 7.10/mm (Zero hour for the attack) at M.G. emplacement N.13.b.05.35 and houses at N.19.b.10.65. Z/46 Trench Mortar Battery fired 41 rounds on enemy wire and front line trench about N.7.a.95.70. Owing to an operation of Y/46 Group Battery, 46th D.A. requiring the assistance of Z/46 Trench Mortar Battery, Operation Order No.104 was issued altering the time of relief between Z and Y/46 Trench Mortar Batteries until 5am. on 30/6/17.	
do.	29/6/17.		Y/46 Heavy Trench Mortar Battery fired 7 rounds on trench at N.13.c.75.20.65	

Army Form C. 2118.

WAR DIARY
or
INTELLIGENCE SUMMARY.
46th Div. Heavy and Medium T.M. Batteries.

(Erase heading not required.)

Instructions regarding War Diaries and Intelligence Summaries are contained in F. S. Regs., Part II. and the Staff Manual respectively. Title pages will be prepared in manuscript.

Place	Date	Hour	Summary of Events and Information	Remarks and references to Appendices
Bully Grenay	29/6/17		N.13.c. 85.40 by request of Infantry. 2/46 Trench Mortar Battery fired 10 rounds in wire cutting at N.7.a with good effect.	
	30/6/17		X/46 Heavy Trench Mortar Battery and X/46 Trench Mortar Battery did not fire. Y/46 Trench Mortar Battery fired 45 rounds on trenches at N.7.a. 90.65 and N.7.a. 98.45 in support of operations on the right. 2/46 Trench Mortar Battery fired 41 rounds on enemy sap N.7.b. 10.40 and houses in N.7.6. at request of Infantry. Capt. L.R. Mowas M.C. proceeded on Course today and Capt N. Giblin, O.C. Y/46 Heavy Trench Mortar Battery took up the duties of Divisional Trench Mortar Officer.	

W Giblin
Captain R.F.A.
A.D.T.M.O. 46th Division.

CONFIDENTIAL.

WAR DIARY.

Trench Mortar Batteries.

JULY 1st: to JULY 31st: 1917.

Army Form C. 2118.

WAR DIARY
or
INTELLIGENCE SUMMARY.

46th Divisional Heavy and Medium Trench Mortar Batteries.

(Erase heading not required.)

Place	Date	Hour	Summary of Events and Information	Remarks and references to Appendices
Sains-env. Ecoivres.	1/7/17.		Y/46 Heavy & X/46 Medium Trench Mortar Batteries did not fire.	
	2/7/17.		Y/46 Trench Mortar Battery fired 45 rounds during the early morning at N.7.a.90.65 and N.7.a.98.45. Trench Mortar Batteries did not fire during this period as Infantry dispositions were not clearly defined.	
	3/7/17.		V/46 Heavy Trench Mortar Battery did not fire. Y/46 Trench Mortar Battery fired 20 rounds this morning on enemy Trenches N.7.a.90.65 with good effect. Lieut G.P. Clay proceeded on 10 days leave to England. One 9.45 inch Heavy Trench Mortar returned to Ord. Party. Y/46 Trench Mortar Battery fired 10 rounds on enemy trench at N.7.a.9.7 (NARWAL). Other Batteries did not fire by request of O.C. 5th Canadian Infantry Brigade.	
	4/7/17.		Canadians resuming completion of relief. 2/Lieut 16. H. Kain with D.A.C. joined V/46 Heavy Trench Mortar Battery for attachment. 2/Lieut JH Ruddock, 231 Brigade R.F.A joined Z/46 Trench Mortar Battery for attachment. 2/Lieut C.J.	

WAR DIARY or INTELLIGENCE SUMMARY

Army Form C. 2118.

46th Divisional Heavy and Medium Trench Mortar Batteries.

Place	Date	Hour	Summary of Events and Information	Remarks and references to Appendices
Sains-en-Gohelle	4/7/17		Aldridge, 230th Brigade R.F.A. joined V/46 Trench Mortar Battery for attachment.	
	5/7/17		V/46 Heavy Trench Mortar Battery fired 18 rounds during the morning on enemy strong point, trenches and railway cutting in X.13 central. Considerable damage appeared to be done and material was thrown up. Y/46 Trench Mortar Battery fired 50 rounds during the afternoon on enemy trenches between N.7.a.90.40 and N.7.a.90.60 to knock the enemy considerable damage was done. Enemy retaliated with medium minenwerfer without damage. Operation Order No. 105 issued ordering the relief of personnel of the 46th Divisional Artillery now manning the Heavy and Medium Trench Mortars by personnel from the 2nd Canadian Divisional Artillery on 8/7/17, relief to be completed by 5.0 a.m. 9/7/17. On completion of relief personnel will return to the 46th Divisional Ammunition Column by 10/7/17. One Heavy Trench Mortar Emplacement handed over to Second Army.	

WAR DIARY or INTELLIGENCE SUMMARY

Army Form C. 2118.

466 Divisional Heavy and Medium Trench Mortar Batteries

Place	Date	Hour	Summary of Events and Information	Remarks and references to Appendices
Sains en Gohelle	6/7/17		Y/46 Heavy Trench Mortar Battery fired 20 rounds at 11.30am on trenches and wire south of railway cutting from N13c 70.90 to N13c 80.50 with good effect. Y/46 Trench Mortar Battery fired 50 rounds during the afternoon of the 5th in counter preparation to enemy trench mortars, considerable damage being caused to enemy trenches and losses from N7a 90.60 to N7a 95.40.	
"	7/7/17		Y/46 Heavy Trench Mortar Battery fired 25 rounds at 11.0am on railway cutting N13a 90.00 to N13c 60.90 and trench from N13c 60.90 to N13c 90.50. Good damage was done, many direct hits being obtained on cutting and trench. Y/46 Trench Mortar Battery fired 110 rounds during the afternoon and evening of 6/7/17, on enemy trenches and wires between N7a 90.60 and N7a 95.40 with excellent effect. The enemy retaliated vigorously. Relief of batteries by 2nd Canadian Division	
"	8/7/17		No firing done. Relief of batteries by 2nd Canadian Division Trench Mortars completed at 4.30pm. Four heavy trench mortars handed over to W/2c Heavy Trench Mortar Battery and all effective	

Army Form C. 2118.

WAR DIARY
or
INTELLIGENCE SUMMARY.

46th Divisional Heavy and Medium Trench Mortar Batteries

(Erase heading not required.)

Place	Date	Hour	Summary of Events and Information	Remarks and references to Appendices
Sains-en-Gohelle	8/7/17		Heavy and Medium ammunition handed over. Personnel of Heavy and Medium Trench Mortars withdraws to billets in Bully Grenay.	
Boyeffles	9/7/17		Office of the Divisional Trench Mortar Officer moved to Chateau-BOYEFFLES. Personnel of Heavy & Medium Trench Mortars marched to billets at HOUCHIN.	
do.	11/7/17		Personnel of Trench Mortar Batteries spent the morning in cleaning guns and equipment.	
do.	12/7/17		Capt. N. Gilkin of D.T.M.O. proceeded on 10 days leave to England. Lieut. C. Balmes took up the duties of D.T.M.O. during his absence. During the morning personnel had an inspection of small arms ammunition and gas drill.	
do.	13/7/17		Rifle and Marching Drill carried out in the morning and Semaphore Signalling during the afternoon.	
do.	14/7/17		Batteries paraded at 9.0am for Route March under the O.C. D.T.M.O. Batteries and returned to Camp at 11.0 am.	
do.	15/7/17		Lieut. J.H. Waddingham and 5 ORs from Medium Batteries proceeded	

Army Form C. 2118.

WAR DIARY
or
INTELLIGENCE SUMMARY.
(Erase heading not required.)

464 Divisional Heavy Trench Mortar Bttry.
(and Medium Trench Mortar Bttrs.)

Instructions regarding War Diaries and Intelligence Summaries are contained in F. S. Regs., Part II. and the Staff Manual respectively. Title pages will be prepared in manuscript.

Place	Date	Hour	Summary of Events and Information	Remarks and references to Appendices
Beuffles	15/7/17		on a course in the new Trench Newton Trench Mortars at the Trior Army Trench Mortar School. The Course lasts 5 days.	
do.	16/7/17		Rifle and Marching drill carried out during the morning, and afternoon was spent in Gas Helmet inspection and drill. Semaphore Signalling and a lecture by Officers Commanding Batteries in Map Reading.	
do.	17/7/17		Batteries carried out a Route March during the afternoon.	
do.	18/7/17		Rifle and Marching drill carried out during the morning, and also instructions in Morse with Buzzer Key given.	
do.	19/7/17		Batteries paraded at 9.0am for Route March under the O/D.T.M.O. returning to camp at noon. Semaphore signalling carried out during the afternoon and also Batteries received instructions in Field Map Reading.	
do.	20/7/17		Rifle and Marching Drill carried out during the morning and Revolver practice during the afternoon.	
do.	21/7/17		Route March carried out by Batteries from 9.0am until noon.	

Army Form C. 2118.

WAR DIARY
or
INTELLIGENCE SUMMARY. 46th Divisional Heavy and Medium Trench Mortar Batteries.

(Erase heading not required.)

Place	Date	Hour	Summary of Events and Information	Remarks and references to Appendices
Boyeffles	22/7/17		Inspection of tents and equipment. Church Parade at 6.30 p.m.	
do.	23/7/17		During the night of 22nd, the camp was visited by hostile aircraft. One bomb was dropped in close proximity to the tents. 2 O.R.'s (V/46 Heavy Trench Mortar Battery) were killed, and 4 O.R's (V/46) and 1 O.R. (Z/46) wounded. 2/Lieut. L. Zioli proceeded on 10 days admitted to hospital. 2/Lieut. L. Zioli proceeded on 10 days leave to England. Medium Trench Mortar Batteries carried out Gun drill and Heavy Trench Mortar Battery carried out Semaphore Drill.	
do.	24/7/17		Batteries proceeded on Route March under the orders of the A/D.T.M.O. at 9.0 a.m. & returned to Camp at noon. Fatigue parties for the Divisional Ammunition Column were provided during the afternoon.	
do.	25/7/17		Medium Trench Mortar Batteries carried out Gun drill and Heavy Trench Mortar Battery Squad drill. Also practice for all Batteries with Lectures in Field Map reading.	

Army Form C. 2118.

WAR DIARY
or
INTELLIGENCE SUMMARY

4th Divisional Heavy and Medium Trench Mortar Bties.

(Erase heading not required.)

Place	Date	Hour	Summary of Events and Information	Remarks and references to Appendices
Boyelles	26/7/17		During the morning, Rifle, Marching and Saluting Drill was carried out by all Batteries and Semaphore Signalling for all ranks during the afternoon.	
do.	27/7/17		A route march under the orders of the A/DTMO was carried out by all Batteries during the morning. Fatigue parties were provided for the Divisional Ammunition Column during the afternoon.	
do.	28/7/17		Capt. C. R. Munro M.C. returned from leave and took up his duties of DTMO. Capt. N. Gillin returning to the command of the Heavy Battery. Lieut. G. P. Clay and 15 O.R's from the Medium Trench Mortar Battery proceeded to the First Army Trench Mortar School on a five days course in the 6 inch Trench Mortar. Capt. N. Gillin proceeded on D.T.M.O's leave.	
do.	30/7/17		Marching, Rifle and Saluting Drill carried out by all Batteries. Fatigue parties were provided for the Divisional	

Army Form C. 2118.

WAR DIARY
or
INTELLIGENCE SUMMARY.
46th Divisional Heavy and Medium Trench Mortar Batteries.

(Erase heading not required.)

Place	Date	Hour	Summary of Events and Information	Remarks and references to Appendices
Boyeffles	30/7/17		Ammunition Column during the afternoon.	
	31/7/17		All Batteries took part in 2 inch Gun Drill.	
	31-7-17			

A. Williams
Captain R.F.A.
D.T.M.O 46th Division.

CONFIDENTIAL.

WAR DIARY.

TRENCH MORTAR BATTERIES.

AUGUST 1st: to AUGUST 31st: 1917.

Army Form C. 2118.

WAR DIARY
or
INTELLIGENCE SUMMARY.
(Erase heading not required.)

46th Div. Heavy and Medium T.M. Batteries

Place	Date	Hour	Summary of Events and Information	Remarks and references to Appendices
Boyeffles	1/8/17		All Batteries paraded at 9.0 am for Route March, under the D.T.M.O. and returned to Camp at 10.15 am. Casualties - NIL.	
do.	2/8/17		Captain C.R. Mounas, M.C. proceeded on 10 days leave to England. Lieut. J.H. Waddingham M.C. took over the duties of D.T.M.O. Batteries provided personnel for fatigues at Divisional Ammunition Column. Casualties - 1 O.R. (V/46 T.M. Bty.) and 1 O.R. (Z/46 T.M. Bty.) accidentally wounded by revolver shot and admitted to hospital.	
do.	3/8/17		During the morning Batteries carried out Semaphore Signalling and Guns and Gun stores were cleaned and laid out for inspection. The afternoon was spent in Gun Drill and fatigues. Casualties - NIL.	
do.	4/8/17		All Batteries paraded at 9.0 am for Route March. Casualties - NIL.	
do.	5/8/17		Lieut. C. Balme and 2/Lieut. G.P. Clay returned to duty from a course at First Army Trench Mortar School. Lieut C. Balme took over the duties of D.T.M.O. and Lieut. J.H. Waddingham M.C. returned to the command of Z/46 Trench Mortar Battery. Casualties :- NIL.	

Army Form C. 2118.

WAR DIARY
or
INTELLIGENCE SUMMARY. 46th Div. Heavy and Medium T.M. Batteries
(Erase heading not required.)

Instructions regarding War Diaries and Intelligence Summaries are contained in F. S. Regs., Part II. and the Staff Manual respectively. Title pages will be prepared in manuscript.

Place	Date	Hour	Summary of Events and Information	Remarks and references to Appendices
Boyelles	6/8/17		Rifle and Marching Drill under Officers was carried out during the morning and afternoon was spent in fatigues. Casualties – NIL.	
do.	7/8/17		Batteries were practiced in map reading and lectures on compass and protracts. Afternoon was spent in fatigues. Casualties – NIL.	
do.	8/8/17		Batteries paraded at 9.0 am for Route March, returning to camp at 10.15 am. Casualties – NIL.	
do.	9/8/17		Batteries took part in Gun Drill and Semaphore Signalling. Casualties – NIL.	
do.	10/8/17		Rifle and Marching Drill under N.C.O's and fatigue party was provided during the afternoon for the Divisional Ammunition Column. Casualties – NIL.	
do.	11/8/17		Batteries paraded at 9.15 am for Route March and returned to Billets at 10.30 am. Casualties – NIL.	
do.	12/8/17		Lieut. J. H. Waddingham, N. C. paraded at Headquarters, 46th Divisional Artillery, Boyelles to receive medal ribbon presented by Major General Thwaites, C.B., Commanding 46th Division.	

Army Form C. 2118.

WAR DIARY
or
INTELLIGENCE SUMMARY.
(Erase heading not required.)

46th Div. Heavy and Medium T.M. Batteries.

Instructions regarding War Diaries and Intelligence Summaries are contained in F.S. Regs., Part II. and the Staff Manual respectively. Title pages will be prepared in manuscript.

Place	Date	Hour	Summary of Events and Information	Remarks and references to Appendices
Boyeffles	13/8/17		During the morning Gun Drill in Box respirators was carried out and also Rifle and Marching drill. Casualties. NIL.	
do.	14/8/17		All batteries were taken in 2inch gun drill and Field Map reading with use of Compass and Protractor. Casualties NIL.	
do.	15/8/17		Batteries paraded at 9.0 am for Route March. Casualties NIL.	
do.	16/8/17		All batteries were taken in 2inch gun drill and Semaphore Signalling. Casualties NIL.	
do.	17/8/17		Batteries paraded for Musketry drill, Rifle and Marching drill at 10.30am. Casualties NIL.	
do.	18/8/17		Batteries paraded at 9.15 am for Route March, returning to Billets at 10.30 am. Remainder of morning was spent in Gun and Gun Stores cleaning. Casualties NIL.	
do.	20/8/17		Medium Trench Mortar drill from 9.15 am to 10.15 am and Rifle and Marching drill from 10.15 to 11.15 am. Casualties NIL.	
do.	21/8/17		X/46 Trench Mortar Battery attached to Divisional Ammunition Column for 1 week. 10 ORs (R.A) Heavy and 10 ORs (R.A) Medium Batteries were transferred to Divisional Ammunition Column for a corresponding number of ORs drawn from the Reserve Trench Mortar Personnel. Casualties NIL.	

Army Form C. 2118.

WAR DIARY
or
INTELLIGENCE SUMMARY.
(Erase heading not required.)

46th Div. Heavy and Medium T.M. Btties.

Instructions regarding War Diaries and Intelligence Summaries are contained in F. S. Regs., Part II. and the Staff Manual respectively. Title pages will be prepared in manuscript.

Place	Date	Hour	Summary of Events and Information	Remarks and references to Appendices
Boyeffles	23/8/17		Gun drill in Bore respirators was carried out during the morning and Field Map reading. Casualties Nil.	
do.	24/8/17		Musketry Course for all Batteries from 9-15 to 11-15 am. Casualties Nil.	
do.	25/8/17		Musketry Course for all Batteries from 9-15 to 11-15 am. Casualties Nil.	
do.	27/8/17		Office of Divisional Trench Mortar Officer moved from Boyeffles to Bethune. Batteries remaining at Houchin.	
Bethune	28/8/17		Operation Order No. 211 received from 46th Divisional Artillery ordering one 2 inch Trench Mortar Battery to relieve Y5 Trench Mortar Battery in action (Cambrin Sector) by 4 am 30th August. Casualties - Nil.	
do.	29/8/17		Z/46 Trench Mortar Battery moved from Houchin and relieved Y5 Trench Mortar Battery.	
do.	3/8/17		V/46 Trench Mortar Battery relieved W/46 Trench Mortar Battery in action. X/46 Trench Mortar Battery relieved 2 inch Battery of 66 Div. Artillery in Hulluch Sector. Casualties - Nil.	

A. Munro
Captain R.F.A.
D.T.M.O. 46th Division.

CONFIDENTIAL.

WAR DIARY.

46th: TRENCH MORTAR BATTERIES.

SEPTEMBER 1st: to SEPTEMBER 30th: 1917.

WAR DIARY
or
INTELLIGENCE SUMMARY

Army Form C. 2118.

46th Div. Heavy and Medium T.M. Batteries.

Place	Date	Hour	Summary of Events and Information	Remarks and references to Appendices
Bethune	1/9/17		Orders issued as to the relief of Medium T.M. Batteries with 6th Division on 2/9/17. Casualties Nil.	
"	2/9/17		Relief of 6th Division Trench Mortar Batteries completed. Y/5 Trench Mortar Battery remaining under 6th Division and 1 Officer and 14 ORs of V/2 Heavy Trench Mortar Battery attached to V/46 Heavy Trench Mortar Battery, both manning the Cambrin Sector. Casualties Nil.	
Sailly Labourse	3/9/17		Offr. of Divisional Trench Mortar Officer moved from Bethune to Sailly Labourse. Casualties Nil. X/46 Trench Mortar Battery fired 20 rounds in counter offensive to enemy trench mortars and caused them to cease fire. Y/46 Trench Mortar Battery fired 51 rounds into enemy wire between H.7.c. 02.30 and C.12.a. 96.57 with good effect. Y/5 Trench Mortar Battery fired 32 rounds at enemy tent line about A.38.c. 10.85 in counter offensive to enemy trench mortars with good results. Casualties Nil. V/46 Heavy Trench Mortar Battery fired in counter offensive	
do.	4/9/17			continued.

Army Form C. 2118.

WAR DIARY
or
~~INTELLIGENCE SUMMARY.~~ 46th Div. Heavy and Medium T.M. Batteries

(Erase heading not required.)

Place	Date	Hour	Summary of Events and Information	Remarks and references to Appendices
Sailly Labourse	4/9/17		to enemy trench mortars. Y/46 Trench Mortar Battery fired 16 rounds on enemy dug outs at H.13.c.70.90 and silenced it. In support of a proposed raid by 138th Infantry Brigade Y/46 Trench Mortar Battery fired 33 rounds in wire cutting. At nearest of infantry Y/5 Trench Mortar Battery fired 55 rounds in wire cutting at A.28.c.20.70 and between G.W.b.35.60 and G.W.b.35.85 with good effect although no gaps are visible yet. Owing to a premature round during the above 1 OR of this Battery was killed.	
do.	5/9/17		At request of infantry Y/46 Heavy T.M. Battery silenced an enemy trench mortar firing from A.28.a.33.15. Y/46, Z/46 and Y/5" Trench Mortar Batteries were employed in wire cutting in support of the proposed raid on 138th Infantry Brigade front. Casualties Nil.	
do.	6/9/17		Y/46 Trench Mortar Battery continued wire cutting on the front of the proposed raid. The wire here is very thin and gave	

WAR DIARY or INTELLIGENCE SUMMARY

Hght. Brit. Heavy and Medium T.M. Batteries.

Army Form C. 2118.

Place	Date	Hour	Summary of Events and Information	Remarks and references to Appendices
Noielles s/Labourse	6/9/17		cut in places. German 2nd line wire impossible to see except in one place. Z/46 and Y/5 Trench Mortar Batteries were also employed in wire cutting. Casualties - Nil.	
	7/9/17		Y/46 Heavy T.M. Battery had a destructive shoot on Houses about H.7.c. 25.40 and every trench mortar at H.7.c. 42.49. One house was completely demolished. Y/46 Trench Mortar Battery fired 120 rounds into enemy wire in front of 1st and 2nd lines to 138th Infantry Brigade raid. Front line wire was destroyed in many places as far as could be seen. Second line wire appeared to be damaged where observation was possible. Y/5 Trench Mortar Battery were also employed in wire cutting. Casualties :- 4 ORs (Y/46) and 4 ORs (Z/46) gassed and admitted to hospital while loading tents in VERMELLES. Y/46 T.M. B.H. position at DUDLEY LANE was blown in by enemy heavy trench mortar.	
	8/9/17		Y/46 Trench Mortar Battery fired and silenced enemy trench mortar at H.7.c. 40.45 and also during the raid by 138th	continued.

WAR DIARY
or
INTELLIGENCE SUMMARY
46th Div. Heavy and Medium T.M. Batteries.

Army Form C. 2118.

Place	Date	Hour	Summary of Events and Information	Remarks and references to Appendices
Sailly Labourse	8/9/17		Infantry Brigade. In support of the raid X/46 Trench Mortar Battery fired 103 rounds at enemy machine guns at H.13.a. 30.30, H.13.a. 30.60 and H.13.a. 30.45 and at 12.0 midnight at enemy trench mortars at H.13.a. 62.10 and H.13.c. 60.81 and silenced them. Y/5 Trench Mortar Battery enlarged gaps in enemy wire between A.28.c. 06.92 and A.28.c. 45.67, and also between G.4.c. 40.70 and G.4.c. 40.30. Z/46 T.M. Battery fired on machine guns and trench mortars in E.5.a. in conjunction with the raid. 1 mortar of Y/46 T.M. Battery was destroyed by enemy trench mortar and some ammunition was blown up. Order No. 106 issued in regard to moving of back billets from Sailly Labourse to Noyelles. Casualties Nil.	
do.	9/9/17		Y/46 Heavy T.M. Battery silenced an enemy trench mortar firing from H.13.d. 53.60. X/46 Trench Mortar wire at H.13.a. 20.70. A good gap is reported by the Infantry. Y5.7 T.M. B'y was enlarged in widening gaps already cut. Y/46 T.M. B'y fired 67 rounds at enemy wire on the front to be raided by	

WARDIARY
INTELLIGENCE SUMMARY. 46th Div. Heavy and Medium T.M. Batteries.

Army Form C. 2118.

Place	Date	Hour	Summary of Events and Information	Remarks and references to Appendices
Sailly	9/9/17		138th Infantry Brigade. Front Line wire cut. Casualties NIL.	
Laurette contd. do.	10/9/17		V/46 Heavy T.M. By. fired 7 rounds at H.13.d.71.65 with very good effect. Ammunition was blown up and concrete dug out shattered. X/46 T.M. By. fired several times between 9.30 a.m and 5.30 a.m in counter offensive to hostile mortar and Infantry reported enemy mortar was silenced each time. Y/5 T.M. By. fired on enemy wire at A.27.b.80.48 with good effect. Casualties 10R killed and	
do.	11/9/17		1 OR wounded by a premature round. Y/5 T.M. By. V/46 Heavy T.M. By. fired in counter offensive to hostile trench mortar and silenced it. In accordance with St Elie Group O.O. No.4. V/46 Battery fired on A.28.a.23.28 and A.28.a.60.42. Whilst firing on A.28.a.90.72 in counter offensive to hostile trench mortar the position was shelled with about 20 10.5 cm's	
do.	12/9/17		but did no damage. At 10.30 a.m on 12th V/46 Battery fired 12 rounds at "GOOSE". Two direct hits were obtained on top of "GOOSE" position. Enemy retaliated with 15 cm's for 3 or 4 hours on our position getting a direct hit and putting 1 gun	

WAR DIARY
or
INTELLIGENCE SUMMARY. 46th. Div. Heavy and Medium T.M. Batteries.

Army Form C. 2118.

Place	Date	Hour	Summary of Events and Information	Remarks and references to Appendices
Sailly Labourse	12/9/17.		Out of action. Y/5 T.M. Battery fired 55 rounds on enemy front line with good effect as part of Artillery programme. Raid down by the 138th Infantry Brigade raid. Y/5 Trench Mortar Battery came out of action and returned to 5th Division. Z/46 Trench Mortar Battery took over Caubrin front. Y/46 Trench Mortar Battery taking over Z/46 Battery's front. 2/Lieut. C.F. Aldridge attached Y/46 T.M. Battery prepared on each Trench Mortar course at 1st Army Trench Mortar School. Casualties Nil.	
do.	13/9/17.		V/46 Heavy Trench Mortar Battery registered a house at E.12.C.72.70. X/46 Trench Mortar Battery fired on enemy wire at M.13.C.53.45 and night patrols report "wire loose and easily penetrated at points." Y/46 and Z/46 Trench Mortar Batteries carried out wire cutting with good effect. Lieut. J.H. Waddingham M.C. relinquished the command of Z/46 Trench Mortar Battery and was posted to 46th Divisional Ammunition Column. 2/Lieut. H.E. Coombs joined Z/46 Battery for attachment. Casualties Nil.	
do.	14/9/17.		X/46 Trench Mortar Battery fired in counter offensive to enemy trench mortars and also carried out wire cutting.	

Army Form C. 2118.

WAR DIARY
or
INTELLIGENCE SUMMARY.
(Erase heading not required.)

46th Div. Heavy and Medium T.M. Batteries.

Place	Date	Hour	Summary of Events and Information	Remarks and references to Appendices
Sailly Labourse.	15/9/17		Y/46 Trench Mortar Battery fired on enemy trenches about A.22.c. 20.40. A large quantity of timber was blown up. X/46, Y/46 and Z/46 Batteries were employed in wire cutting.	Casualties Nil.
do.	16/9/17		Y/46 Trench Mortar Battery fired on enemy trenches between G.5.c.45.20 and G.5.c. 80.10 doing considerable damage to trenches. Z/46 Battery carried out wire cutting.	Casualties Nil.
do.	17/9/17		X/46, Y/46, and Z/46 Batteries carried out wire cutting with good effect.	Casualties Nil.
do.	18/9/17		Y/46 Heavy Trench Mortar Battery fired 15 rounds on 6' enemy trenches in A.28.a & c. with aeroplane observation. X/46, Y/46 and Z/46 Batteries carried out wire cutting.	Casualties Nil.
do.	19/9/17		Y/46 Heavy Trench Mortar Battery carried out a shoot on Louses at G.6.d. 94.10 and G.6.d. 93.05. Infantry observers reported that a number of the enemy ran into Louses at H.1.c. 00.30.	Casualties Nil.
do.	20/9/17		Y/46 and Z/46 Batteries were relieved by Batteries of the 2nd Division in Cambrin Sector.	Casualties Nil.
do.	21/9/17		Y/46 Heavy Trench Mortar Battery fired on houses at G.6.d. 94.10 partly demolishing two. Also carried out a shoot on enemy trench mortars at G.12.a. 25.80, and G.12.a. 40.75. Observation impossible as trench mortars are in a Quarry but brick and	

Army Form C. 2118.

WAR DIARY
or
INTELLIGENCE SUMMARY

46th Bde. Heavy and Medium T. M. Batteries.

(Erase heading not required.)

Instructions regarding War Diaries and Intelligence Summaries are contained in F. S. Regs., Part II. and the Staff Manual respectively. Title pages will be prepared in manuscript.

Place	Date	Hour	Summary of Events and Information	Remarks and references to Appendices
Souilly Labouse	21/9/17		Trench mortars thrown out. "Casualties NIL.	
	22/9/17		X/46, Y/46 and Z/46 Batteries carried out wire cutting with good effect. Lieut C. E. Walker proceeded on leave to England. Casualties NIL.	
do.	23/9/17		Y/46 Heavy Trench Mortar Battery obtained direct hits on concrete machine gun at H.7.c.60.01. X/46, Y/46, & Z/46 Batteries carried out wire cutting with good effect.	
do.	24/9/17		X/46 Trench Mortar Battery fired on trenches between H.13.a.60.15 and H.13.a.60.30 in counter offensive to hostile trench mortars at request of Infantry. Casualties :- 1 OR (X/46 Battery) killed and 2 ORs (X/46 Battery) wounded, caused by a direct hit on emplacement. 2 OR's (Y/46 Battery) slightly wounded and remained at duty. Two positions were blown in by enemy shell fire but guns were undamaged.	
do.	25/9/17		Y/46 Heavy Trench Mortar Battery fired on enemy trench mortar at H.7.C.45.47. Enemy mortar opened fire at once but ceased after 2 rounds. Shooting was very good and rounds appeared to hit the target. Enemy trench mortar did not fire again. X/46, Y/46 and Z/46 carried out wire cutting. Casualties :- NIL.	

Army Form C. 2118.

WAR DIARY
or
INTELLIGENCE SUMMARY. 46th Div. Heavy and Medium T.M. Batteries.
(Erase heading not required.)

Place	Date	Hour	Summary of Events and Information	Remarks and references to Appendices
Sailly Labourse	26/9/17		Y/46 Heavy Trench Mortar Battery fired 28 rounds at enemy trench mortars at H.7.c.60.65 and H.7.c.45.47. The first mortar was silenced and second emplacement appeared to be badly damaged. Casualties Nil.	
do.	27/9/17.		X/46, Y/46. and Z/46 Batteries carried out wire cutting. Casualties Nil.	
do.	28/9/17.		Y/46 Trench Mortar Battery obtained direct hits on two M.G. emplacements in G.12.a. Casualties Nil.	
do.	29/9/17.		Y/46 Heavy Trench Mortar Battery fired 2 rounds at enemy trench mortar at H.7.c.60.65 and owing to platform jumping no further firing was possible. X/46 and Y/46 Batteries carried out wire cutting. Casualties Nil. 2nd Lieut J.H. Banks wounded on leave.	
do.	30/9/17.		V/46 Heavy Trench Mortar Battery fired 3 rounds at enemy trench mortar at H.7.c.40.45 doing considerable damage. X/46 Trench Mortar Battery destroyed a dugout in sap at H.13.a.25.70. A party of 30 men from 46th Divisional Ammunition Column attached to Trench Mortar Batteries for the purpose of preparing gun pits for the 6 inch mortar.	

D. Skinner.
Captain R.F.A.
D.T.M.O. 46th Division.

CONFIDENTIAL.

WAR DIARY.

TRENCH MORTAR BATTERIES.

OCTOBER 1st: to OCTOBER 31st: 1917.

WAR DIARY or INTELLIGENCE SUMMARY

Army Form C. 2118.

46th Div. Heavy and Medium Trench Mortar Batteries.

Place	Date	Hour	Summary of Events and Information	Remarks and references to Appendices
Sailly Labourse	1/10/17		V/46 Heavy T.M. Battery carried out a shoot against hostile trench mortar doing considerable damage to position. X/46 T.M. Battery fired in counter offensive to enemy trench mortars which were silenced, also into Sap H.13.a.25.70 where a dugout was apparently destroyed. Casualties NIL.	
do.	2/10/17		Y/46 Trench Mortar Battery fired 30 rounds at enemy trench mortar H.13.c.70.80 silencing it and doing considerable damage to position. Y/46 Trench Mortar Battery fired 90 rounds into enemy wire between G.S.C.50.20 and G.S.C.70.15 doing very considerable damage to the wire, another gun being put out about G.S.C.50.20. V/46 Heavy Trench Mortar Battery carried out a destructive shoot against enemy houses at G.6.d.90.40 and trench junction at G.6.d.50.30 and G.6.d.43.22. Direct hits were obtained on houses partly demolishing them and considerable damage was done to trenches. Casualties NIL. X/46 Heavy Trench Mortar Battery fired at enemy trench mortars at G.12.a.46.70 and G.12.a.30.80 but observation of shoot was impossible.	
do.	3/10/17		X/46 Trench Mortar silenced an enemy trench mortar at H.13.a.70.30 and also on Coy. HQ at H.13.a.70.65 where a large amount of debris was thrown up. I got in enemy wire was also cut at H.13.a.20.70. Casualties NIL. Z/46 T.M. Bty. received one 6 inch Newton trench Mortar.	

Army Form C. 2118.

WAR DIARY
or
INTELLIGENCE SUMMARY.
(Erase heading not required.)

46th Div. Heavy and Medium Trench Mortar Battery

Place	Date	Hour	Summary of Events and Information	Remarks and references to Appendices
Sailly Labourse	4/10/17		V/46 Heavy Trench Mortar Battery fired 10 rounds at enemy trench mortar at H.7.c.45.50, doing considerable damage to trenches round position and also 14 rounds were fired at houses between H.7.a.60.05. and H.7.a.20.50. Direct hits were obtained on houses doing very considerable damage. Enemy trench mortar opened fire that was silenced after three rounds. X/46 Trench Mortar Battery fired 40 rounds at enemy trench mortar at H.13.a.60.40 and by H.Q. at H.13.a.70.65, doing considerable damage, timber etc. being thrown up. Enemy retaliated vigorously, apparently this is a tender spot. Y/46 Trench Mortar Battery were employed in wire cutting. Three explosions were caused in enemy front line probably bomb dumps. Casualties :- 1 O.R. (2n46.T.M.By) wounded.	
do.	6/10/17		V/46 Heavy Trench Mortar Battery fired 5 rounds on C.6.d.45.18 with good effect. X/46 Trench Mortar Battery fired 50 rounds at enemy trench mortar at H.13.a.70.20 and silenced it. A barrage was also put down in H.13.c.40.65, enemy trench mortar at H.13.d.80.00 and enemy front line H.13.c.55.70 to H.13.c.60.50 in support of the daylight raid. Infantry reported barrage effective.	

WAR DIARY
or
INTELLIGENCE SUMMARY.

Army Form C. 2118.

With 9. Heavy and Medium T.M. Batteries.

Place	Date	Hour	Summary of Events and Information	Remarks and references to Appendices
Sailly Labourse (contd.)	6/10/17		In support of 138th Infantry Brigade daylight raid Y46 T.M. Battery fired 136 rounds on 6 German trior and second lines on the front of the raid. Front line was badly knocked about and what could be seen of the second line was destroyed. Casualties Nil.	
do.	7/10/17		127 rounds were fired by Y46 Trench Mortar Battery which was about G.12.c.50.85 and G.12.c.45.95 doing very considerable damage, and also on 6 German trior line during the daylight raid. Casualties Nil.	
do.	8/10/17		Y46 Heavy Trench Mortar Battery fired 10 rounds at enemy trench mortar at G.12.b.80.70 at request of Infantry. A large amount of material was blown up. Also 21 rounds were fired on enemy trenches from G.12.b.70.50.6 G.12.c.82.35 in conjunction with 138th Infantry Brigade raid. On enemy trench mortars at H.13.a.67.67 was also silenced by X/46 Trench Mortar Battery. Casualties Nil.	
do.	9/10/17		Y46 Heavy Mortar Battery fired 50 rounds at enemy trench mortars at H.7.c.40.45 and G.12.b.75.80 with good effect, a large amount of timber being thrown up. Trenchettes repaired 6 x 46 Trench Mortar Battery who's enemy trench mortars were annoying him, his Battery promptly engaged the T.M's with very good effect. Casualties :- 1OR (Y/46 Tm.By) accidentally wounded.	

Army Form C. 2118.

WAR DIARY
or
INTELLIGENCE SUMMARY.

(Erase heading not required.)

46th Divisional Heavy and Medium T.M. Batteries.

Place	Date	Hour	Summary of Events and Information	Remarks and references to Appendices
Sailly Labourse	10/10/17		X/46 Trench Mortar Battery carried out wire cutting. Several shells were blown in but no gap made. Y/46 Trench Mortar Battery fired bombs at enemy wire in G.12.b.2.4 and G.12.b.3.3 where a good gap was made.	
do.	11th and 12/10/17		X/46 Trench Mortar Battery dispersed an enemy working party between H.13.c.48.70 and H.13.c.45.00 reported by Jummellers. Y/46 Trench Mortar Battery carried out wire cutting with good effect and fired on an enemy T.M. position between at G.12.a.92.27, direct hits being obtained.	
do.	13/10/17		Casualties :- 1 O.R. (Y/46 Tm.Bty.) accidentally injured. V/46 Heavy Trench Mortar Battery fired 28 rounds on 6 houses about G.12.b.75.80 doing considerable damage, direct hits repeatedly obtained. 30 ORs attached from I.T.C. having finished building the 6 inch positions for Z/46 Battery, proceeded to build for X/46 Battery, in HUGOLANE. Z/46 T.M. Battery fired 10 rounds with 6 inch trench mortar with good effect. This is the first time a Gun mortar in action has been fired by 46th Division. Three 6 inch trench mortars received from D.A.D.O.S. One 6 inch mortar taken into action. Battery fired 10 rounds into house at G.12.b.90.65 with good effect, the ruins being completely removed.	
do.	14/10/17		Y/46 Trench Mortar Battery fired 47 rounds in connection operations to	

Army Form C. 2118.

WAR DIARY
or
INTELLIGENCE SUMMARY.

(Erase heading not required)

46th Divisional Heavy and
Medium T.M. Batteries.

Place	Date	Hour	Summary of Events and Information	Remarks and references to Appendices
Sailly Laburse	14/10/17		Hostile trench mortars and silenced them. In support of 137th Infantry Brigade raid a good gap was cut in enemy wire & the infantry were able to get through and obtain an entrance. Casualties Nil.	
do.	15/10/17		X/46 and Y/46 Trench Mortar Batteries commenced work on buck positions. V/46 Heavy Trench Mortar Battery fired 15 rounds silo every trench mortar at H.7.c.50.45. and House at H.7.a.20.50. Three direct hits were obtained on House and considerable damage done to enemy trenches. Y/46 Trench Mortar Battery carried out wire cutting. Casualties Nil. One 6 inch mortar taken into action.	
do.	16/10/17		V/46 Heavy Trench Mortar Battery fired at House at H.7.a. 20.50. and crater at H.7.c. 55.01. Four direct hits were obtained on the House doing considerable damage and one direct hit on the crater. Y/46 Trench Mortar Battery did much damage to enemy wire	
do.	17/10/17		between H.7.c. 00.35 and H.7.c. 10.10. Casualties:- 2/Lieut C Nobb wounded & ungassed, one infantryman Heavy trench Mortar Recovery from D.A.D.O.S.	
do.	18/10/17		V/46 Heavy Trench Mortar Battery fired 12 rounds at crater at H.7.c. 55.01. and enemy trench between H.7.a. 10.10 and G.12.b. 90.40 direct hits being obtained. X/46, Y/46 and Z/46 Trench Mortar Batteries carried out wire cutting, with good effect. Casualties Nil.	
do.	19/10/17		Y/46 Heavy Trench Mortar Battery carried out a shoot against	

Army Form C. 2118.

WAR DIARY
or
INTELLIGENCE SUMMARY.
(Erase heading not required.)

46th Divisional Heavy and
Medium T.M. Batteries.

Instructions regarding War Diaries and Intelligence Summaries are contained in F. S. Regs., Part II. and the Staff Manual respectively. Title pages will be prepared in manuscript.

Place	Date	Hour	Summary of Events and Information	Remarks and references to Appendices
Sailly Labourse	19/10/17		Enemy dug outs at H.7.c.30.50 and H.7.c.26.55, doing considerable damage. Y/46 and Z/46 Trench Mortar Batteries carried out wire cutting with very good results. Casualties Nil.	
do.	20/10/17		Medium Trench Mortar Batteries were employed in wire cutting. Casualties Nil.	
do.	21/10/17		V/46 Heavy Trench Mortar Battery fired 15 rounds each every trench between H.7.c.50.20 and H.7.c.70.20 – 7 rounds fell in the trench but extent of damage not known. X/46. Y/46 and Z/46 Trench Mortar Batteries carried out wire cutting with very good effect. Casualties 1 OR (Y/46 T.M. Bty.) wounded. 6 inch Newton mortar received from DADOS, one 6 inch mortar together with ammunition received 8 rounds at concrete OP at V/46 Heavy Trench Mortar Battery fired	
do.	22/10/17		H.7.a.20.50 and houses at H.7.a.25.40, 2 direct hits being obtained on house and large quantity of debris thrown up. X/46 Trench Mortar Battery cut 2 gaps, 5 yards wide in enemy wire about H.15.c.6.6. Y/46 and Z/46 Trench Mortar Batteries were employed in wire cutting. 2 gaps were cut successfully by Z/46 Battery. Y/46 Battery also carried out harassing fire against Quarries in G.12.a. Casualties:- 1 OR (Z/46 T.M. Battery) killed in action.	
do.	23/10/17		V/46 Heavy Trench Mortar Battery carried out a shoot against concrete	

WAR DIARY
or
INTELLIGENCE SUMMARY.

Army Form C. 2118.

46th Divisional Heavy and Medium T.M. Batteries.

Place	Date	Hour	Summary of Events and Information	Remarks and references to Appendices
Sailly Labourse	23/10/17	1.17	O.P. Result of damage could not be seen on account of bad light. X/46 Trench Mortar Battery cut a gap in enemy wire at H.25.b.55.45. and also an existing gap at H.13.a.60.30 was widened. Y/46 Trench Mortar Battery registered a trench mortar and also cut a gap in enemy wire at G.13.6.1.14. Casualties NIL.	
do.	24/10/17		X/46 and Y/46 Trench Mortar Batteries successfully cut gaps in enemy wire at various points. Casualties NIL.	
do.	25/10/17		Y/46 Heavy Trench Mortar Battery carried out a shoot against Concrete O.P. at H.7a.30.50, doing considerable damage to surroundings. X/46 and Y/46 continued wire cutting. Two observation heavy trench mortars returned one new battery heavy trench mortar Y/46 into action. 6 DADOS. Casualties:- 1 OR (X/46) and 1 OR (Y/46) wounded.	
do.	26/10/17		Y/46 Heavy Trench Mortar Battery fired at enemy trench mortar at H.7.a.05.15, a direct hit being obtained, and also destroyed a house at H.7.a.24.50. X/46 T.M. Bty fired 51 rounds on 6 Cross roads at H.19.B.20.10 at request of Infantry, also wire at H.13.a.60.16 where a gap was widened. Y/46 and Z/46 also carried out wire cutting. Casualties 1 OR killed, 1 OR wounded (X/46) 1 Officer wounded (Lieut. G.P. Clay) one trench mortar taken into action.	
do.	27/10/17		X/46, Y/46, and Z/46 Batteries carried out wire cutting successfully	

Army Form C. 2118.

WAR DIARY
or
INTELLIGENCE SUMMARY
(Erase heading not required.)

46th Div. Heavy and Medium T.M. Batteries.

Place	Date	Hour	Summary of Events and Information	Remarks and references to Appendices
Faithy Laterue	27/10/17		with 2 inch and 6 inch Trench Mortars. Casualties Nil.	
do.	28/10/17		One 6 inch mortar taken up in action by V/46 Heavy Trench Mortar Batty. on 6 houses at H.33.c. 10.80 and about N.3.6. 20.80 with good effect. One direct hit obtained on first target and 6 direct hits on the second. This firing was done with the new Mark III mortar. X/46, Y/46 and Z/46 Trench Mortar Batteries continued wire cutting with very good effect. Casualties:- 10R (Y/46 T.M.B?) wounded.	
do.	29/10/17		Y/46 Heavy Trench Mortar Battery fired 25 rounds on 6 houses about H/6. C. 80.15 with good effect, timber and other debris being blown up, and also on 6 enemy Trench mortars at H.7.C. 23.19.J, H.7.C. 43.44 and H.7.C. 30.12. Casualties 10R (Y/46 T.M.B. 39) killed. One 2 inch mortar returned to DADOS.	
do.	30/10/17		Y/46 Heavy Trench Mortar Battery fired on 6 enemy Trench Mortar at H.7.C. 45.49 with good effect, one direct hit being obtained on position and also destroyed a bomb store at H.7.C. 15.71. X/46, Y/46 and Z/46 continued wire cutting, where several good gaps were cut. Casualties Nil. 2 inch mortar taken into Ordnance Depot. New Heavy Trench Mortar received from DADOS.	
do.	31/10/17		Casualties Nil.	

A.R. Munro
Captain R.F.A.
D.T.M.O. 46th Division

CONFIDENTIAL.

WAR DIARY.

TRENCH MORTAR BATTERIES.

NOVEMBER 1st: to NOVEMBER 30th: 1917.

Army Form C. 2118.

WAR DIARY or INTELLIGENCE SUMMARY.

(Erase heading not required.)

46th Div: Heavy and Medium T.M. Batteries.

Place	Date	Hour	Summary of Events and Information	Remarks and references to Appendices
Sailly Labourse	1/11/17		Y/46 Heavy Trench Mortar Battery fired 28 rounds on Loaves at G26.85.60 where a dump appeared to be blown up. Direct Hits were obtained on Loaves and enemy HQ at H.27c.10.85. During 137th Infantry Brigade raid X/46 Trench Mortar Battery engaged enemy trench mortars at H19a.65.70 and H13d.50.60 and enemy trench junctions at H19d.40.80 and H20c.30.70. Z/46 Trench Mortar Battery fired 100 rds of 6 inch into enemy wire about H32d.99.65, a large amount of wire being cut. Casualties :- NIL.	Ref. Map Sheet 1/40 000 36.c.
do.	2/11/17		Y/46 Heavy Trench Mortar Battery carried out a shoot against enemy concrete emplacement at H13d.45.90. A large amount of debris was thrown up. At request of Infantry X/46 Trench Mortar Battery fired into enemy front line in H13a. to silence Priests' bombs. Y/46 Trench Mortar Battery expended 170 rounds in wire cutting with good results. Casualties :- NIL.	
do.	3/11/17		V/46 Heavy Trench Mortar Battery placed our new pattern heavy trench mortar in action, 23 rds. fired by new mortar at enemy trench mortar at H33c.35.42 obtaining a direct hit and enemy strong point at H33a.75.10 but effect could not be seen owing to mist. Y/46 Trench Mortar Battery obtained eight direct Hits on enemy Priests	Mk III

WAR DIARY
or
INTELLIGENCE SUMMARY

Army Form C. 2118.

46th Division Heavy and Medium T.M. Batteries

Place	Date	Hour	Summary of Events and Information	Remarks and references to Appendices
Sailly Labourse	3/11/17.		Mortars about G.12.b.80.60, 2/46 Trench Mortar Battery caused considerable damage to enemy wire about H.32.d.90.20 and H.32.d.95.65 and also silenced an enemy T.M. firing from H.33.a.10.05. Casualties NIL.	Ref map Sheet 1/40,000 36.C.
do.	4/11/17.		1/46 Heavy Trench Mortar Battery fired 15 rounds with new mortar on 6 PUITS 13 and surrounding buildings, considerable damage being done. 20 rounds were also fired at enemy T.M. at N.3.6.20.28 a direct hit being obtained. Casualties :- NIL. 1/46 Trench Mortar Battery damage enemy wire between G.11.b.85.80 and G.5.a.65.02, and also silenced an enemy T.M. Casualties NIL. 2/46 Trench Mortar Battery placed one 6 inch Trench Mortar in action at H.31.d.55.75.	
	5/11/17.		Total rounds fired by Trench Mortar Batteries during preceding week are:- Heavy Battery 156. Medium Battery 1110 rounds. Equalling in weight 36 Tons 7 cwt.	
do.	6/11/17.		1/46 Trench Mortar Battery fired 20 rounds at enemy concrete emplacement at H.13.b.72.68 doing considerable damage. 1/46 and 2/46 carried out wire cutting successfully. Two 6 inch Trench Mortars drawn from I.T.M.O.S. Casualties NIL.	

Army Form C. 2118.

WAR DIARY
or
INTELLIGENCE SUMMARY.
(Erase heading not required.)

46th Division Heavy and Medium T.M. Batteries.

Place	Date	Hour	Summary of Events and Information	Remarks and references to Appendices
Sailly Labourse	7/11/17.		1/46 Trench Mortar Battery fired 15 rds at FOSSE 13 in H.7.a. One direct hit was obtained on FOSSE, 6 on slag heaps and 1 small dump was blown up just on right of FOSSE. 1/46 Trench Mortar Battery cut a gap in enemy wire at H.25.b.50.60 and also fired 17 rounds at enemy trench mortar at H.25.b.57.32 obtaining direct hits. 31 rounds of such were also fired by same Battery at enemy wire at H.19.a.90.80 and wire was cleared. 1/46 and 2/46 Trench Mortar Batteries continued wire cutting cutting several gaps. During the shoot of 2/46 Battery the enemy retaliated with 77m.m. 4.2's and medium trench mortars. Casualties:- 1 O.R. (1/46 T.M. By.) wounded.	By map Sheet 1/40,000 36.C.
do.	8/11/17.		Infantry reported to 1/46 Trench Mortar Battery enemy M.G. firing from house at H.7.a.60.06. 12 rounds were fired into it, and a great deal of debris was thrown up. 2 gaps were cut in enemy wire about H.25.d.70.90 and H.19.a.95.80 by 1/46 Trench Mortar Battery. 1/46 Trench Mortar Battery engaged enemy trench mortar at G.12.b.47.20, damaging earthworks. 2/46 Trench Mortar Battery also engaged enemy T.M. emplacement at H.33.c.1.8 and H.33.c.25.70 doing considerable damage.	

WAR DIARY
or
INTELLIGENCE SUMMARY. 46th Divisional Heavy and Medium T.M. Batteries

Army Form C. 2118.

(Erase heading not required.)

Place	Date	Hour	Summary of Events and Information	Remarks and references to Appendices
Sailly Labourse contd.	8/11/17		One 9.45 inch (MK III) mortar drawn from 94 D.O.S. C.R.T. inspected Heavy and Medium trench mortar positions in Loos sector. Work was commenced on ESSEX LANE Position for 9.45 inch (MK III) mortar. Casualties:- 1 OR (X/46 Bty) wounded and since died in hospital. Y/46 Heavy Trench Mortar Battery fired 16 rounds on fences between N.3.C.40.10 and N.3.C.65.35. Fences partly demolished.	Ref. map. Sheet 1/40.000 36.C.
do.	9/11/17		4 bombs observed to fall through the rags of 6 fences. X/46 Trench Mortar Battery fired 35 rounds into enemy wire between H.25.C.55.50 and H.25.C.60.50, a gap being cut. Y/46 Trench Mortar Battery damaged enemy trench in G.12.b. Z/46 Trench Mortar Battery registered N.2.b.80.95 and H.32.d.85.88. Three 2 inch trench mortars returned to D.T.M.O.D in place of 6 inch. 2/Lieut J.W. Edge returned from leave. 2/Lieut. G. Liston, acting as Liaison Officer to Loos Crown moved his headquarters to Railway Alley. C.R.T. inspected trench mortar positions in Loos sector. Casualties:- 1 OR (X/46 Bty) wounded.	
do.	10/11/17		In support of 11th Division raid Y/46 Heavy Trench Mortar Battery fired 10 rounds with good effect on to N.3.a.52.52.	

WAR DIARY
or
INTELLIGENCE SUMMARY.
(Erase heading not required.)

Army Form C. 2118.

46th Division Heavy and Medium Trench Mortar Blies

Instructions regarding War Diaries and Intelligence Summaries are contained in F. S. Regs., Part II. and the Staff Manual respectively. Title pages will be prepared in manuscript.

Place	Date	Hour	Summary of Events and Information	Remarks and references to Appendices
Sailly Laurette	10/11/17 contd.		Y/46 Trench Mortar Battery fired 100 rds burst on to light railway at G.12a.28.35. One piece of rail was seen to go up, also an enemy trench mortars at G.12a.2.5.27 and G.12a.34.29. A direct hit was obtained on the latter and two explosions caused. During 11th Division raid Z/46 Trench Mortar Battery fired 59 rounds 6 inch with good effect on to enemy machine guns at H.32.d.85.88 and H.32.d.90.07. and railway cutting at N.2.C.80.97. Lieut. C.T. Aldridge returned from Rear Station and resumed command of Z/46 Trench Mortar Battery. The 3rd 6 inch mortar of Z/46 T.M. Battery was taken into action. Casualties - NIL	Ref. map Sheet 1/40.000 36.c.
do.	11/11/17		V/46 Heavy Trench Mortar Battery fired 9 rounds at houses at H.7a.62.32 and H.7a.68.35. Much debris being thrown up. At request of infantry X/46 Trench Mortar Battery silenced an enemy M.G. firing from H.13a.60.30. Also 40 rounds at enemy front line wire from H.13a.40.30 to H.13a.55.25. The enemy trench was very badly knocked about and wire smashed up and cleared. Y/46 Trench Mortar Battery fired 72 rounds 2 inch at enemy wire G.12.c.65.00 to G.12.c.8.9.	

WAR DIARY
or
INTELLIGENCE SUMMARY

Army Form C. 2118.

466 Division Heavy and Medium T.M. Batteries.

Place	Date	Hour	Summary of Events and Information	Remarks and references to Appendices
Sailly Labourse	11/11/17		Wire was very badly damaged and one explosion caused in enemy trench about G.12.c. 65.05. New wire at G.12.d. 38.97 was destroyed. Telephone communication of 2/46 T.M. Battery was destroyed by enemy shell fire, but was again restored by evening. Two 2 inch trench mortars were returned to D.T.M.O.S. Casualties - Nil.	Ref. map Sheet 1/40,000 36.C.
do.	12/11/17		Y/46 Heavy Trench Mortar Battery fired 9 rounds into houses at N.3.c. 30.30 obtaining 4 direct hits, also 5 rounds on house at H.33.c. 10.80, and 10 rounds at concrete OP at H.13.d. 45.92. X/46 Trench Mortar Battery obtained two direct hits on enemy trench mortar at H.20.c. 60.40. Y/46 Trench Mortar Battery fired 136 rounds in harassing fire under orders received from Corps. Z/46 Trench Mortar Battery fired into enemy wire between H.26.c. 90.30 and H.26.d. 05.35. with good effect. Casualties. Nil. Y/46 Heavy Trench Mortar Battery fired 10 rounds at dugouts	
do.	13/11/17		in BOIS DE DIX HUIT (H.B.26). Some timber was blown up but visibility was poor. X/46 Trench Mortar Battery silenced enemy trench mortar firing from H.13.a.60.30 at request of Infantry. 30 rds. 6 inch were fired at H.13.a. 40.30. Wire was seen to be blown	

WAR DIARY
or
INTELLIGENCE SUMMARY
(Erase heading not required.)

Army Form C. 2118.

46th Division Heavy and Medium T.M. Batteries.

Place	Date	Hour	Summary of Events and Information	Remarks and references to Appendices
Sailly Laurette centre.	13/11/17		up and also direct hits were obtained on trench. Blowing up trench carried. Y/46 Trench Mortar Battery silenced enemy heavy trench mortar firing from G.6.c. 88.36. Also completely destroyed a medium trench mortar firing from G.12.b. 42.20, all kinds of debris being thrown up. A gap was also cut at G.12.b. 45.10. Enemy post at G.12.b. 52.10 was also engaged and trench was knocked in and considerable amount of timber was thrown up. Trench junction at G.12.a. 90.33 was badly damaged. Z/46 Trench Mortar Battery commenced building a new position for trench mortar. O.R.A. inspected the Heavy and medium trench mortars in Houllach Sector. Casualties Nil.	Ref. map sheet 1/40,000 36.C.
do.	14/11/17		V/46 Heavy Trench Mortar Battery fired 20 rounds at enemy trench mortar at H.19.d. 85.32 with good effect. x/46 and y/46 Trench Mortar Batteries carried out wire cutting successfully. Y/46 Battery also engaged enemy trench mortars at G.6.d. 97.46 and G.12.b. 30.40 doing considerable damage to earthworks about positions and into GAMBIT ALLEY between G.12.d 40.95 and G.12.b. 70.60, many direct hits being obtained & considerable damage done to trench. R.S.M. Lee J.G. V/46 Heavy Trench Mortar Battery was despatched to the Base Depot HAVRE owing to there being no establishment for a R.S.M. in a Heavy Trench Mortar	

Army Form C. 2118.

WAR DIARY
or
INTELLIGENCE SUMMARY.
(Erase heading not required.)

46th Division Heavy and Medium T.M. Batteries.

Place	Date	Hour	Summary of Events and Information	Remarks and references to Appendices
Sailly Labourse	14/11/17		Battery. Sergt. Suckerham G Y/46 Trench Mortar Battery transferred to Trench Mortars H.Q. Staff vice B.S.M. Lee to Base. G.R.H. inspected the Heavy and Medium trench mortars in ST. ELIE sector. Casualties - Nil.	Ref. map sheet 1/40.000 36c.
do.	15/11/17		Y/46 Trench Mortar Battery fired on enemy dump at H1c 73.85 and houses at H1c 75.15 to H7a 73.85 obtaining some direct hits and completely destroying houses. X/46 Trench Mortar Battery engaged and silenced an enemy trench mortar firing from H13a 65.30. An enemy infantry post at H19a 80.25 was also fired on by this Battery and trench boards and timber were seen to be blown up. 30 rounds of 6 inch were fired at enemy wire at H13d 25.35. Wire was badly broken up and is quite easy of access. Numerous direct hits were obtained on enemy trench G12.a.7.4 to G.12.b.5.1 and enemy wire around G12.b. 30.25 by Y/46 Trench Mortar Battery. Z/46 Trench Mortars was engaged in cutting enemy wire & gap was successfully cut measuring from H32d 95.65 to H32d 95.55. This Batter also obtained 2 direct hits with 6 inch trench mortar on enemy Lewis mortar at H33c 20.85. Court of Enquiry held at Sailly Labourse H.Q. to enquire into the circumstances under which 2/Lieut Ford W. of X/46 Trench Mortar Battery was wounded on night of 8/9th Nov.	

Army Form C. 2118.

WAR DIARY
or
INTELLIGENCE SUMMARY.
(Erase heading not required.)

46th Division Heavy and Medium T.M. Batteries

Place	Date	Hour	Summary of Events and Information	Remarks and references to Appendices
Sailly Labourse	15/11/17		G.R.A. inspected trench mortar positions in Loos sector. Casualties NIL.	
do.	16/11/17		V/46 Heavy Trench Mortar Battery fired 8 rounds on enemy trench junction at H.13.d.26.71 with good effect and one direct hit put up a quantity of wood. Also engaged an enemy O.P. at H.13.b.90.70. Ref. map Sheet 1/40000 36.c. but no direct hits were obtained. Good hits were obtained on houses at H.7a.26.35, much debris being thrown up. Road junction at H.34.a.1.3 was registered. X/46 Trench Mortar Battery fired on enemy H.Q. at approx. H.13.a.50.30 with good effect. Trench boards were seen to be blown up and trench badly knocked about. Gap 10 yds wide was also cut in enemy wire at H.13.c.60.40. Z/46 Trench Mortar also cut a gap in enemy wire at H.26.c.8.7 by his Battery. V/46 Heavy Trench Mortar Battery had an ignited prematurely burst in a No. 1 III Trench mortar whilst firing charges and bomb were about 6. — continued over →	

Army Form C. 2118.

1/46 Heavy and Medium
T.M. Battery.

WAR DIARY
or
INTELLIGENCE SUMMARY.
(Erase heading not required.)

Place	Date	Hour	Summary of Events and Information	Remarks and references to Appendices
Sailly Labourse	16/11/17		O.C. leading. 3 men were slightly burnt. 20 Infantry men attached from 138th Infantry Brigade commenced work on Tunnel position for 1/46 Trench Mortar Battery.	Ref. map Sheet 1/40.000 36.c.
do.	17/11/17		1/46 Heavy Trench Mortar Battery carried out a shoot in accordance with Toc Emp. OO26. 15 rounds in Salvos about H13.c. 95.57. several Lay demolished houses being destroyed, and large amount of debris thrown up. Direct hits were also obtained on HAMLET trench at G12.c. 70.65, G12.c. 90.35, H7a. 50.02, and H7c. 90.60. A trench mortar firing from H7c. 44.48 was also silenced. 1/46 Trench Mortar Battery cut a gap in enemy wire at H25.c. 47.85 and other wire was considerably damaged. 2/46 Trench Mortar Battery fired 12 rounds 6 inch on H33.a 70.10 in accordance with Toc Emp. OO26. Two direct hits were also obtained on enemy trench mortar at H26.c. 80.60. 1/46 Trench Mortar Battery put one 6 inch mortar in action in GORDON ALLEY position. Casualties NIL	
do.	18/11/17		1/46 Heavy Trench Mortar Battery fired 10 rounds on Schoolhouse at N13.c. 65.80. large amount of debris was thrown up around building. 10 rounds were fired on HAMLET trench (H7d). direct hits being obtained	

WAR DIARY
or
INTELLIGENCE SUMMARY

Army Form C. 2118.

466 Division Heavy and Medium T.M. Batteries.

Place	Date	Hour	Summary of Events and Information	Remarks and references to Appendices
Sailly Labourse	18/11/17		One round fell in enemy wire at H7d 12.46 cutting a gap. One 9"45" MK III mortar in action was destroyed by a prematers. The cause of the prematers is thought most probable through the charge flashing through a flaw in the bomb. Y/46 Trench Mortar Battery fired 25 rounds on enemy wire H13c 55.30 to H13c 55.10, rounds fell in wire, but damage could not be seen owing to mist. 30 rounds were also fired into enemy wire behind craters H13c 47.97 to H13c 55.55. Y/46 Trench Mortar Battery fired 100 rounds into ZEPPELIN ALLEY between G5d 47.95 and G5d 35.65 doing considerable damage. Z/46 Trench Mortar Battery cut a gap in enemy wire at H7c 10.02 and wire was destroyed at G5c 70.15. Z/46 Trench Mortar Battery cut a gap in enemy wire at H32 b 50.20. Average daily trench mortar expenditure for week ending 9 a.m 19/11/17:- Heavy 29. Medium 220. Casualties:- 1 OR (Y/46 T.M.By.) wounded slightly by premature.	Ref map Sheet 1/40000 36.c.
do.	19/11/17		Y/46 Heavy Trench Mortar Battery fired 6 rounds into HAMLET trench obtaining direct hits at H7d. 20.35 and H7d 15.43, rounds were also	

WAR DIARY
or
INTELLIGENCE SUMMARY.
(Erase heading not required.)

46th Division Heavy and Medium T.M. Batteries.

Army Form C. 2118.

Place	Date	Hour	Summary of Events and Information	Remarks and references to Appendices
Sailly Labourse	19/11/17		also fired on houses about H76.6.43 H.70.73.85 blowing up a large amount of debris. X/46 Trench Mortar Battery cut gap in enemy wire at H.25.6.60.40. and wire was considerably damaged about H.25.6.80.60. Y/46 Trench Mortar Battery fired at enemy trench mortars at G.12.6.40.80 and G.12.6.40.20. 3 direct hits being obtained on the first target. Casualties NIL.	Ref. map Sheet 1/40.000 36.C.
do.	20/11/17		Y/46 Heavy Trench Mortar Battery fired on H.20.C.62.05 under Corps OO.28. Also 10 rounds were fired on enemy trench mortars at H.7.C.43.48 and G.12.6.85.48. 10 rounds were also fired at enemy OP at H.13.d.35.68. considerable damage being done to trench and neighbouring walls. X/46 Trench Mortar Battery fired 11 rounds on trench between H.25.6.59.51 and H.25.6.70.19. doing considerable damage. 1 mortar of this Battery was put out of action by enemy 5.9 battery. One round hit the emplacement and filled the mortar with earth. 55 rounds were fired into enemy trench in H.25.6. under Corps O.O. 28. Y/46 Trench Mortar Battery cut gap in enemy wire at G.12.6. 15.45 and	

Army Form C. 2118.

WAR DIARY
or
INTELLIGENCE SUMMARY.
(Erase heading not required.)

4th Division Heavy and
Medium T. M. Batteries.

Instructions regarding War Diaries and Intelligence Summaries are contained in F. S. Regs., Part II. and the Staff Manual respectively. Title pages will be prepared in manuscript.

Place	Date	Hour	Summary of Events and Information	Remarks and references to Appendices
Ailly Talence	20/11/17		G.2.b.10.45. Also bombarded trenches SLAG ALLEY between G5.b.00.05 and G5.B.20.30 and ZEPPELIN ALLEY about G.5.b.35.75, considerable damage being done to these trenches. Several small explosions were caused at enemy post at G5.c.55.55. 7/46 Trench Mortar Battery fired 75 rounds burst into trench junction H26a.13.07. and trench near direct hits being obtained on trench junction, also trench junction at H26a 13.07 was engaged under Group 0028. X/46 Trench Mortar Battery fired 25 rounds on enemy wire about H19.a.60.90. clearing about 40 square yds. Also registered junction of HILDA and HINDOO trenches. Gordon and Hugo Lane positions were heavily shelled with 4.2's, but no damage was done to mortars and very slight damage done to positions. Mortars remained in action. Casualties NIL.	By map Sheet 1/40000 36.C.
do.	21/11/17		V/46 Heavy Trench Mortar Battery fired 10 rounds into HAMLET trench which appeared to do considerable damage, but observation was difficult owing to mist. 10 rounds fired on houses about H14.a.00.60	

Army Form C. 2118.

WAR DIARY
or
INTELLIGENCE SUMMARY.
(Erase heading not required.)

46th Division Heavy and Medium T.M. Batteries.

Place	Date	Hour	Summary of Events and Information	Remarks and references to Appendices
Sailly Labourse	21/11/17		and H13.6.90.25 doing considerable damage. Y/46 Trench Mortar Battery cut gaps in enemy wire about H19.a.85.20. In support of Infantry raid 30 rounds were fired at midnight on H19a 37.95 and 8 rounds on same target in registration previously; 3 direct hits were obtained. Y/46 Trench Mortar Battery cut a gap in enemy wire at G12.6.12.42 and also caused an explosion at G5c. 55.20. Z/46 Trench Mortar Battery registered successfully enemy trench mortar at H33.a.05.00. Total rounds fired for week ending 9am 22nd. Heavy - 180. Heavy 1481. Total weight 46 tons 12 cwt. Casualties - NIL. Medium 1481. Total weight 46 tons.	Re/map sheet 1/20000 36.C.
do.	22/11/17		Y/46 Heavy Trench Mortar Battery fired 8 rounds at concrete O.P at about H13.6. 72.68. 70 direct hits were obtained but one house just on right of O.P. was demolished 12 rds. These were fired into HULLUCH (H13.6. 72.68 to about H13.a. 50.80). One bomb store was blown up and one house completely demolished. X/46 Trench Mortar Battery fired 30 rounds at enemy wire in H13a with good effect. Y/46 Trench Mortar Battery completely destroyed enemy wire from G12.d. 35.95 to G12.d. 25.95. Also engaged and silenced enemy trench mortar "LEOPARD". Wire at H7.c. 05.10 and G12.a. 35.05 was also destroyed. Z/46 Trench Mortar Battery fired at enemy new trench H32.d.60.90 to H32.d.70.50, and a good percentage of bombs fell in the trench.	

Army Form C. 2118.

WAR DIARY
or
INTELLIGENCE SUMMARY.
(Erase heading not required.)

46th Division Heavy and Medium T. M. Batteries.

Place	Date	Hour	Summary of Events and Information	Remarks and references to Appendices
Sailly Labourse	22/11/17		12 rounds 6 inch were fired at enemy trench mortar in house at H.33.c.35.85. 3 direct hits were obtained on the building. 2/Lt. (Actg Lieut) F. Gillett ceased to command Z/46 Trench Mortar Battery and returned to J.A.C. 2/Lieut J.H. Ruddock posted from X/46 Trench Mortar Battery to Z/46 Trench Mortar Battery, 2/Lieut E.R. Lister 36.C. to the command of Z/46 Trench Mortar Battery.	Ref. map Sheet 1/40000 36.C.
do.	23/11/17		2/Lieut attached Z/46 Battery transferred for attachment to X/46 Battery. G.S.O.I. 46th Division went round left and centre trench mortar positions. Y/46 Heavy Trench Mortar Battery fired 10 rounds on to enemy trench mortar at H.13.a.50.50, house being demolished. 15 rounds on trench junction H.20.c.65.05, direct hits being obtained and considerable damage done. X/46 Trench Mortar Battery cut gap in enemy wire at H.13.a.30.30, and also obtained 2 direct hits on enemy trench mortar at H.13.a.38.40. Y/46 Trench Mortar Battery fired 14 rounds 6 inch into enemy wire at C.12.d.15.95 and between G.5.c.20.35 and G.5.c.25.30, wire being completely destroyed. Z/46 Trench Mortar Battery considerably damaged enemy trench H.32.d.60.90 to H.32.d.70.50, and also obtained 5 direct hits on building at H.33.a.07.00. Casualties Nil.	

WAR DIARY or INTELLIGENCE SUMMARY

Army Form C. 2118.

46th Division Heavy and Medium T.M. Batteries.

Place	Date	Hour	Summary of Events and Information	Remarks and references to Appendices
Sailly Labourse	24/11/17		Y/46 Heavy Trench Mortar Battery fired 11 rounds on Louses in H.7a.80.80 and in H.1c.80.10, one Louse being completely demolished. 10 rds fired at enemy trench mortar (GOOSE) at H.13.a.60.51, all bombs bursting well, two blowing up sapping timbers and trench boards. X/46 Trench Mortar Battery fired 20 rounds at enemy wire in H.18.a.90.10. 2 rds 6 inch fired at enemy wire H.13.c.70.30. After second round mortar was destroyed owing to a premature. Y/46 Trench Mortar Battery cut gap in enemy wire at G.12.a.23.95. Z/46 Trench Mortar Battery fired 20 rounds 6 inch at enemy T.M. emplacement at H.33.a.07.00. Observation for effect was difficult owing to thick undergrowth. Casualties:- 1 OR (X/46 Battery) killed, and 2 ORs (X/46) and 1 OR (Y/46) wounded.	Ref. map Sheet 1/40000 36.C.
do.	25/11/17		Y/46 Heavy Trench Mortar Battery fired 10 rounds at FOSSE 13. in H.7.a. One direct hit was obtained on moment of FOSSE and one Louse was demolished on left of FOSSE. X/46 Trench Mortar Battery fired at enemy wire at approx. H.25.b.55.05 with good effect. Y/46 Trench Mortar Battery fired at enemy wire in front of QUARRIES. (G.12.a.32.07). Also destroyed wire about G.5.c.4.2. Z/46 Trench Mortar Battery cut 2 gaps in enemy wire at H.32.b.5.3 and H.32.b.60.05	

WAR DIARY
or
INTELLIGENCE SUMMARY.
(Erase heading not required.)

Army Form C. 2118.

46th Division Heavy and Medium T.M. Batteries

Place	Date	Hour	Summary of Events and Information	Remarks and references to Appendices
Sailly Labourse	25/11/17		Smoke was seen issuing from chimneys of houses at N.3.a.75.70. 2/46 Battery fired 8 rounds burst at the houses and obtained 3 direct hits.	Ref. map Sheet 40000 36.C.
do.	contd. 26/11/17		1/46 Heavy Trench Mortar Battery fired 10 rounds at houses from H.7.a.80.80 to H.1.c.80.10 by order of Genjr. One partly demolished house was completely destroyed. 10 rds fired at enemy trench mortar at about H.13.a.70.85. It is difficult to locate this T.M. position, but 2 rounds blew up a great deal of timber and debris. X/46 Trench Mortar Battery cut got 10 yards wide in enemy wire at H.25.6.80.40. Y/46 Trench Mortar Battery destroyed enemy wire at following places:- H.13.a.10.93, G.2.B.80.65, G.2.B.40.30, G.12.a.90.30, G.12.a.55.20. Also engaged enemy T.M's firing from G.12.a.75.20 and G.12.6.50.20. This battery also engaged and destroyed machine gun emplacement at G.5.C.61.45 and believed to have knocked out periscope at G.5.C.10.46. Z/46 Trench Mortar Battery engaged enemy H.Q. at H.33.a.2.8. All bombs fell within 30 yds. of target. Observation was difficult owing to house immediately in front of target. This house was partly destroyed by 2 direct hits. 35 rounds 6 inch fired at enemy wire from H.32.B.4.4 to H.32.d.75.75. Wire was cleared leaving no considerable obstacle excepting odd stakes & loose ends.	

WAR DIARY or INTELLIGENCE SUMMARY

(Erase heading not required)

Army Form C. 2118.

46th Division Heavy and Medium Trench Mortar Batteries.

Place	Date	Hour	Summary of Events and Information	Remarks and references to Appendices
Sailly Labourse	26/10/17		Z/46 Trench Mortar Battery put their Trench Mortar in action. V/46 Heavy Trench Mortar Battery fired 10 rounds at Loos about H7a.80.80, H7c.80.10 and H1c.80.10 and demolished one house. X/46 and Y/46 Trench Mortar Batteries carried out wire cutting with good effect. A quantity of timber was thrown up by Z/46 Trench Mortar Battery firing on H33c.35.87. J.T.M.O. 46th Division and J.T.M.O. C.D.A.	Ref. map Sheet 40.000 36.C.
	27/10/17		O.C. V/C.D.A. Battery went to look over trench mortar positions on Hill 70 Sector, and reliefs were arranged for section of V/46 Heavy Trench Mortar Battery and Z/46 Trench Mortar Battery with Battery of 5th Canadian Sine Artillery. Hulluch Road 9.45 inch mortar temporarily out of action though pit being damaged by S.G. This Battery suffered 2 hours shelling but mortar itself was undamaged. Casualties Nil.	
do.	28/10/17		V/46 Heavy Trench Mortar Battery fired 5 rounds on light railway junction at H14.a. 06.48 and obtained one direct hit. Y/46 Trench Mortar Battery damaged enemy wire at G.2.d. 35.90, G.5c. 65.18 and G.5.c. 40.20. and fired in counter operaise on M.G. G.5c. 65.40. and T.M. at G.5.c. 20.65 and Grenades at G.2.a. 40.45. Total rounds fired for week ending 9am 29th:- Heavy 116, Medium 1328. Total weight 39tons 12 cwt.	

Wt. W12839/M1293. 4/50,000. 1/17. D.D. & L., Ltd. Forms/C2118/14.

WAR DIARY
or
INTELLIGENCE SUMMARY

Army Form C. 2118.

466 Division Heavy and Medium T.M. Batteries.

Place	Date	Hour	Summary of Events and Information	Remarks and references to Appendices
Sailly Labourse	28/10/17		MkII. One 9.45 inch Trench mortar put in action in HULLUCH Tunnel Position. One 9.45 inch MkI. taken out from this position. 2/Lieut E.H. Wells joined Trench Mortar Batteries from 7th Hoks & Dubs. Regt and is attached to Y/46 Trench Mortar Battery. Z/46 Trench Mortar Battery was relieved in action in Loos Sector by a Medium Battery of 5th Canadian Div. Artillery. Four 6 inch mortars complete were handed over.	Ref. map sheet 1/40000 36.c.
do.	29/10/17		Y/46 Heavy Trench Mortar Battery in Loos Sector in action. V/46 Heavy Trench Mortar Battery in Loos Sector was relieved in action by Heavy Trench Mortar Battery of 5th Canadian Div. Artillery. One 9.45" mortar (MkIII) less piece mounting and platform handed over. Casualties. NIL. Y/46 Heavy Trench Mortar Battery destroyed two emplacements at H.36.b. 20.20. X/46 Trench Mortar Battery cut a gap in enemy wire at H.13.a. 20.50. Y/46 Trench Mortar Battery engaged enemy trench mortars at G.5.d. 00.30, G.5.d. 05.85, G.5.c. 80.67 with good effect. Casualties :- 2 ORs. (Y/46 T.M. Bty) wounded.	
do.	30/10/17		Y/46 Heavy Trench Mortar Battery obtained 2 direct hits on trench mortar at H.20.c. 52.30. X/46 Trench Mortar Battery cut a gap 7 yards wide in enemy wire at H.13.a. 20.50. Y/46 Trench Mortar Battery obtained	

WAR DIARY
or
INTELLIGENCE SUMMARY
(Erase heading not required.)

Army Form C. 2118.

46th Division Heavy and Medium T.M. Batteries.

Place	Date	Hour	Summary of Events and Information	Remarks and references to Appendices
Sailly Laurette	30/11/17 Contd		Several direct hits on trench mortar emplacement in G.5.d, G.12.b, and G.12.a. Gordon Alley trench mortar position fairly destroyed by shell fire. No casualties to personnel. Trench Mortar boat killed at NOYELLES was shelled at 9.20/m and a direct hit was obtained on men's mess, although no one was in at the time. Also N.C.O.'s mess was hit. Casualties 4 ORs (2 1/46 and 2 x/46) wounded. Total no. of rounds fired during month:- Heavy 642. Medium 5731. Total weight fired - 17 tons 48 cwt. Total casualties during month:- 1 OR killed, 16 ORs wounded. (2 died of wounds and 3 remained at duty.)	Ref. map sheet 1/40000 36.c.
	1/12/1917.			

J. Cromer
Captain R.F.A.
S.T.M.O. 46th Division

46th. Divisional Artillery.
_____

WAR   DIARY

DECEMBER - 1917.

46th. Divisional Trench Mortar Batteries.

WAR DIARY or INTELLIGENCE SUMMARY

Army Form C. 2118.

46th Division Heavy and Medium Trench Mortar Batteries.

Place	Date	Hour	Summary of Events and Information	Remarks
Sailly Labourse	1/12/17		Y/46 Heavy Trench Mortar Battery fired 15 rounds at M.G. at H.W.C. 65.10 (S.E. side of HULLUCH) obtaining a direct hit, and also on water supply at M.W. b. 50.32 (BENIFONTAINE) with good effect. X/46 Trench Mortar fired 6 smoke bombs as an experiment, proving successful, wire was also destroyed in front of trenches on west side of HULLUCH. Y/46 Trench Mortar Battery engaged several enemy trench mortars around CITÉ ST ELIE and the Quarries with good effect and with good results in front line trench on west side of CITÉ ST ELIE. Y/46 Trench Mortar Battery put one 6 inch mortar in action at G06.90.80 (GORDON ALLEY). A section of Y/46 Battery relieved a section of W/25 Battery in action in CAMBRIN sector, taking over 1 Mark III and 2 Mk I mortars. Z/46 Battery relieved Z/25 Battery in action in CAMBRIN SECTOR taking over 4.2" and 4. 6" (out of action) Casualties - NIL.	
do.	2/12/17		Y/46 Heavy Trench Mortar Battery fired 4 rounds into LES BRIQUES (A236.40.70) and various houses and Church at BENIFONTAINE. HULLUCH. X/46 Trench Mortar Battery fired 8 rounds into enemy wire in front of enemy front line N. of BOIS HUGO. Y/46 Trench Mortar Battery fired 20 rounds into QUARRIES (G.12.C.) in night firing and registration. 2/Lieut B.C.V. Wildman, 6th Nott & Derby Regt. joined X/46 Trench Mortar Battery for attachment, 2/Lieut J.K. Saul rejoined 5K Nots & Derby Regt. Casualties NIL.	

Army Form C. 2118.

WAR DIARY
or
INTELLIGENCE SUMMARY.
(Erase heading not required.)

46th Division Heavy and Medium Trench Mortar Batteries.

Instructions regarding War Diaries and Intelligence Summaries are contained in F.S. Regs., Part II. and the Staff Manual respectively. Title pages will be prepared in manuscript.

Place	Date	Hour	Summary of Events and Information	Remarks and references to Appendices
Sailly Labourse	3/12/17		V/46 Heavy Trench Mortar Battery fired 12 rounds at enemy trenches from H20a. 4.2. 95. to H20a. 55.90. (S. of HULLUCH). 6 direct hits were obtained on trenches. 4 rounds fell on slag heap of PUITS No.13 Bis. and 2 rounds fell at H14c 4.2.18 hitting up a quantity of timber. 32 rounds fired into CORONS DE MAROC. Heavy trench mortar was observed firing from here and one at once silenced. Three other heavy TM's and artillery retaliated heavily on our front line and round the gun pit. 6 rounds were fired at enemy trench mortar at A28.C. 10.35 (S. of LES BRIQUES). Enemy retaliated heavily on our front line with 4.2s, 5.9s and heavy trench mortars. 6 rounds were fired in counter offensive at enemy trench mortar at A28.G. 30.30 (S. of LES BRIQUES). X/46 Trench Mortar Battery completely destroyed enemy wire from H13a. 25.50 to H13a. 30.35 (enemy front line trench W. of HULLUCH). Y/46 cut a gap in enemy wire at G12d. 95.35 (trench S.W. of CITÉ ST. ELIE). 25 rounds were also fired at enemy new work in front line S. of QUARRIES, in registration. Z/46 Trench Mortar Battery fired 60 rounds at enemy trenches S. of CORONS DE MAROC in counter offensive to hostile trench mortar. 2/Lieut. C. Liston proceeded on 14 days leave. Casualties: NIL.	
do.	4/12/17		Y/46 Heavy Trench Mortar Battery fired 20 rounds in a destructive shoot on LES BRIQUES (A28.6. 35.70). All rounds fell within close proximity of target, boards being thrown up. Enemy retaliated heavily with 4.2s, but all rounds fell well over position. 10 rounds were fired	

A.093. Wt. W1285/M1293. 750,000. 1/17. D.D. & L. Ltd. Forms/C2118/4.

WAR DIARY or INTELLIGENCE SUMMARY

Army Form C. 2118.

46th Division Heavy and Medium Trench Mortar Batteries.

Place	Date	Hour	Summary of Events and Information	Remarks and references to Appendices
Sailly Labourse	4/12/17		At LOOOS in HULLUCH 6 direct hits were obtained and haves demolished. Smoke was seen issuing from enemy trench bordering southern edge of HULLUCH. X/46 Trench Mortar Battery cut several gaps in enemy wire in front of enemy trench N. of BOIS HUGO, wire was completely destroyed from H13a.25.50 to H13a.30.35 (W. of HULLUCH). 5 rounds also fired into enemy front line and foot at H13a.25.30 in counter offensive action to by infantry. Y/46 Trench Mortar Battery fired 65 rounds into enemy wire at H7c.05.25, cutting a gap and causing an explosion (enemy front line N.W. of HULLUCH). 4 do 6" were fired at enemy trench mortars at G.12a.75.25 and G.12a.80.30 (QUARRIES, W. of CITÉ ST ELIE) with good effect. An enemy T.M. firing from G.12b.57.72 (western outskirts of CITÉ ST.ELIE) was neutralized. The following targets were also fired on with very good effect:- New work at G.12a.65.05 Snipers post at G.12a.50.20 and enemy wire at G.12a.20.30. (Enemy second line W. of CITÉ ST.ELIE). Capt. N. Gillin proceeded on 14 days leave to England. Z/46 Trench Mortar Battery moved their back billets from NOYELLES to ANNEQUIN. Casualties:- NIL.	
do.	5/12/17		Y/46 Heavy Trench Mortar Battery demolished houses at H14.a.15.56 and H14.a.30.70. (BENIFONTAINE), and silenced enemy trench mortar firing from A22c.48.40 (W. of AUCHY-LEZ-LA-BASSE). X/46 Trench Mortar cut several gaps in enemy wire between H25.6.80.50 and H25.6.85.20 (N. of BOIS HUGO) also destroyed wire between H13a.26.50 and H13a.35.25 (outskirts of HULLUCH)	

WAR DIARY or INTELLIGENCE SUMMARY

Army Form C. 2118.

46th Division Heavy and Medium Trench Mortar Batteries.

Place	Date	Hour	Summary of Events and Information	Remarks and references to Appendices
Sailly Labourse	5/12/17 Contd.		6 direct hits were obtained on enemy/post at H13a.30.50 (HULLUCH) and also a trench slide was blown up at H25.b.85.20 (enemy front line N. of BOIS HUGO) Y/46 Trench Mortar Battery destroyed enemy wire between G.2.d.95.35 and H7c.05.20 (Enemy front line N.W. of HULLUCH). A gap was also cut at H7c.07.06 (enemy second line S. of CITÉ ST. ELIE) C.R.F. 46th Division inspected trench mortar positions on CAMBRIN front). Casualties:- NIL.	
do.	6/12/17		Y/46 Trench Mortar Battery fired 10 rounds at tunnel entrance at H14c.36.20 (S.W. outskirts of HULLUCH), considerable debris being thrown up. 6 direct hits were obtained on LES BRIQUES (A28.c). X/46 Trench Mortar Battery widened existing gap in enemy wire between H13a.25.32 and H13a. 30.50 (W. of HULLUCH), and also destroyed enemy wire at H25.b.70.60, H25.b.78.50 and H25.b.85.40 (enemy front line wire N. of BOIS HUGO) Y/46 Battery destroyed enemy wire from H7c.05.20 to H7c.05.15 (between CITÉ ST. ELIE and HULLUCH). Z/46 Battery carried out a destructive shoot on enemy trench junction at G.4.d.70.88, G.4.b.92.00 and enemy trench mortar at G.4.d.99.92 (S. of CORONS DE MAROC). Lieut. G.G. Clay returned from leave and re-assumed command of Y/46 Battery. Casualties:- 1 O.R. (Y/46) wounded, but remained at duty.	
do.	7/12/17		Y/46 Battery obtained a direct hit on buildings at H14c. 10.45 (HULLUCH) knowing a quantity of timber. Also obtained 3 direct hits on	

WAR DIARY or INTELLIGENCE SUMMARY.

Army Form C. 2118.

46th Division Heavy and Medium Trench Mortar Batteries

(Erase heading not required)

Place	Date	Hour	Summary of Events and Information	Remarks and references to Appendices
Sailly Labourse card.	7/12/17		LES BRIQUES (A28.b.). demolishing house. 10 rounds were also fired on enemy trench mortar at A28.a. 65.48. (enemy second line W. of LES BRIQUES) Effect appeared good, considerable timber being thrown up. X/46 Trench Mortar Battery destroyed enemy wire from H25.b.60.60 to H25.b.67.50. (N. of BOIS HUGO). Also obtained 3 direct hits on enemy trench mortar at H26.a. 20.65 (N. of BOIS HUGO), and silenced it. Gaps were also enlarged in enemy wire between H13a.20.65 and H13a. 25.90. (W. of HULLUCH) Y/46 Battery destroyed enemy wire about G12.d. 95.40 and G12d. 45.85. At the latter place an explosion was caused, probably hand bombs. Z/46 Battery engaged enemy trench junctions at G.S.c. 00.88 and G.4.d. 95.95. (S. of CORONS DE MAROC.) and enemy trench mortar at G.4.b. 88.10. (CROSS TRENCH). X/46 Battery placed one 6 inch mortar in action in SEVENTH AVENUE. Casualties :- NIL	
do.	8/12/17		V/46 Battery fired 19 rounds into buildings at LES BRIQUES. House demolished. An enemy trench mortar firing from A.28.C. 88.06 (L. of MAD POINT). was silenced. In support of infantry patrol X/46 Battery fired 30 rounds at enemy trench at H13.a. 62.20 (W. of HULLUCH). Owing to enemy shell fire communication were destroyed at this Battery. Y/46 Battery considerably damaged enemy wire from G12.d. 90.50 to G.12.d. 75.75 and also cut a gap at G12.d. 30.90. Enemy front line N.W. of HULLUCH. Z/46 Battery engaged several active trench mortars around CORONS DE MAROC in counter offensive. Casualties :- NIL.	

Army Form C. 2118.

WAR DIARY
or
INTELLIGENCE SUMMARY
(Erase heading not required.)

46th Division Heavy and Medium Trench Mortar Batteries

Place	Date	Hour	Summary of Events and Information	Remarks and references to Appendices
Sailly Labourse	9/12/17		Y/46 Battery fired at enemy T.M. at A.28.a.65.48. (near LES BRIQUES), in enemy counter offensive. Visibility very bad. X/46 Battery fired at enemy wire at H.25.b.80.50. to H.25.b.60.80. Wire was cut and much bloom about, and also damaged wire between H.19.a.90.80 and H.13.c.60.10. Visibility bad. (S. of HULLUCH). Y/46 Battery destroyed enemy wire from G.12.d.75.75 to G.12.d.65.80. (S.W. of CITE ST. ELIE) Active hostile trench mortars at G.12.b.45.20 and G.12.a.90.30 (between QUARRIES and CITE ST. ELIE) were engaged and silenced. Z/46 Battery engaged enemy trench mortar emplacements at G.4.b.88.10 and G.4.d.99.92 (S. of CORONS DE MAROC), and engaged and silenced active hostile trench mortars at G.12.b.45.20 and G.12.a.90.30 (between QUARRIES and CITE ST. ELIE.) Casualties NIL	
do.	10/12/17		Y/46 Battery demolished house at H.7.a.50.60. (CITE ST. ELIE) Concrete O.P. at H.13.6.90.67 was engaged (HULLUCH). A quantity of debris was thrown up. 8 direct hits were obtained on LES BRIQUES, in A.28.b. Much debris being thrown up. Trench junctions at A.28.a.90.90. A.28.b.12.98. and A.22.c.94.10. were engaged, obtaining 3 direct hits. (Around LES BRIQUES.) X/46 Battery cut enemy wire from H.25.b.60.50 to H.25.b.60.80. (1000 yds N.W. of Bois HUGO) and also between H.19.a.90.80 and H.13.c.60.10 (immediately S. of HULLUCH). Y/46 Battery cut a gap in enemy wire at G.12.b.10.40 (between QUARRIES and CITE. ST. ELIE), and also destroyed wire from G.12.d.40.90 and G.12.d.20.90 (enemy front line in front of CITE. ST. ELIE.) Z/46 Battery carried out a destructive shoot on H.Q POINT (A.28.d.00.13) and enemy front line adjacent to it. (W. of CORONS DE PEKIN). Casualties N/L.	

Army Form C. 2118.

WAR DIARY
or
INTELLIGENCE SUMMARY
(Erase heading not required).

46th Division Heavy and Medium Trench Mortar Batteries.

Place	Date	Hour	Summary of Events and Information	Remarks and references to Appendices
Sailly Labourse	11/12/17		V/46 Battery registered successfully enemy trench junction at G.12.6.70.58. (CITE ST ELIE.) Also obtained a direct hit on enemy TM at H13d.40.50 (HULLUCH). In accordance with 1st Elie Group O.O.2O V/46 Battery engaged enemy trench junction at G.12.6.70.58 (CITE ST ELIE). Much debris was thrown up when firing on enemy TM at A.28.6.22.24 (near LES BRIQUES). Enemy retaliated with 4.2s. X/46 Battery cut a gap in enemy wire between HERRING and HICKS trenches and also destroyed enemy wire in H.13a. In accordance with Special order from Right Battalion Commander Y/46 Battery cut again in enemy wire at H.7c.05.20 (S. of CITE ST ELIE), and in accordance with 2nd Elie Group 0.0.20 85.do were at trench G.26.6.5.05 (500 yds S.W. of CITE ST ELIE) and GAMBIT ALLEY. Z/46 Battery successfully engaged enemy TMs at G.4.6.86.28 and G.4.6.88.10 (W. of CORONS DE MAROC) trench junctions at G.S.c.00.88 and G.4.d.99.92 were engaged. Casualties - NIL	
do.	12/12/17		Enemy Trench mortars firing from H.7d. 20.43 (between CITE ST ELIE and HULLUCH) at K Shaft O.P. was successfully silenced by V/46 Battery 10 rounds were also fired at tunnel entrance at H.14c. 53.10 (eastern outskirts of HULLUCH) Impossible to see results of damage owing to entrance being on far side of slag heap. 12 rounds were fired at LES BRIQUES road running on outskirts. 14 hits were obtained on houses and on trench beside road.	

Army Form C. 2118.

WAR DIARY
— of —
INTELLIGENCE SUMMARY. 46th Division Heavy and Medium Trench Mortar Batteries.

(Erase heading not required.)

Place	Date	Hour	Summary of Events and Information	Remarks and references to Appendices
Sailly Labourse	12/12/17 contd		X/46 Battery fired 40 rounds on enemy wire between HERRING and HICKS, causing considerable damage. Y/46 Battery caused considerable damage from G.12.a.90.33 to G.12.a.70.45 (QUARRIES) Z/46 Battery engaged hostile trench mortars with good results. Casualties :- 1 OR (X/46 Battery) wounded but remained at duty.	
do.	13/12/17		Y/46 Battery engaged enemy machine gun at H14.c.52.02 (southern edge of HULLUCH) 3 rounds falling very close to emplacement. 10 rounds were fired into houses about H7a.60.20 (CITE ST.ELIE) 3 houses were destroyed. Also LES BRIQUES was fired on, & considerable debris was thrown up. X/46 and Y/46 Batteries engaged several enemy trench mortars around QUARRIES and BOIS HUGO in retaliation asked for by Infantry. Z/46 Battery carried out a destructive shoot on enemy trench mortar at A28.c.40.99 (N.W. of CORONS DE MAROC) and trench junction in A28.c and G.4.b. G.R.T. inspected trench mortar positions in ST.ELIE Sector. Z/46 Battery had one 6 inch pit in BARTS ALLEY destroyed by enemy shell fire. Casualties:- NIL.	
do.	14/12/17		Y/46 Battery obtained 2 direct hits on enemy O.P. at H13b.90.70 (HULLUCH) An enemy trench mortar at H7a.30.35 reported active by F.O.O. of X/231 Battery R.F.A. was silenced.	

WAR DIARY
or
INTELLIGENCE SUMMARY

Army Form C. 2118.

46th Division Heavy and Medium Trench Mortar Batteries

(Erase heading not required.)

Place	Date	Hour	Summary of Events and Information	Remarks and references to Appendices
Sailly Labourse	14/12/17 contd.		X/46 Battery destroyed enemy wire in front of HULLUCH trench (H.26.d.). Y/46 Battery engaged enemy trench mortars in vicinity of CITÉ ST ELIE with good result. Z/46 Battery engaged active hostile trench mortars around CORONS DE MAROC and also several trench junctions in same area. One 6 inch mortar of this battery was successfully registered on LES BRIQUES. C.R.A. inspected trench mortar positions on HULLUCH front. Ammunition recess of 6 inch pit of Y/46 Battery partially destroyed by enemy trench mortar. Casualties :- 2 ORs. (Y/46 T.M. Bty.) wounded and admitted to hospital.	
do.	15/12/17		Y/46 Battery fired 5 rounds at LES BRIQUES, and engaged every trench mortar at R.28.a.62.42. (S.W. of AUCHY-LEZ-LA-BASSÉE). Every trench mortar between CITÉ STELIE and HULLUCH was also engaged successfully, enemy retaliating lightly on our position but no damage was caused. Y/46 and Z/46 Batteries also engaged several active hostile trench mortars and in most cases causing considerable damage. Lieut. J.H. Ruddock proceeded on leave. 2/Lieut. E.J. Hollis took over command of Z/46 Battery. Casualties NIL.	
do.	16/12/17		Y/46 Battery engaged enemy T.M. at H.13.6.60.85 (HULLUCH) and obtained 2 direct hits, and also engaged enemy T.M. at H.7.a.90.65. (N.of HULLUCH) X/46 Battery destroyed enemy wire in front of every second line and trenches in H.13.a. (W. of HULLUCH). A bomb store was blown up here. Y/46 Battery did considerable	

WAR DIARY or **INTELLIGENCE SUMMARY.** 46th Division Heavy and Medium Trench Mortar Batteries.

Army Form C. 2118.

Place	Date	Hour	Summary of Events and Information	Remarks and references to Appendices
Sailly Labourse	16/12/17 contd		damage to enemy trench mortars in action between QUARRIES and CITÉ ST. ELIE. Z/46 Battery carried out a destructive shoot on enemy trench junctions S. (CORONS DE MAROC.) Capt Lenahan R.F.A and one Sergeant from First Army School of Mortars attached to V/46 Battery for a fortnight's instruction. Casualties NIL.	
do.	17/12/17		V/46 Battery carried out a shoot on PITS 13. 3 direct hits on ironworks & PIT and slag heap were obtained, & one bomb close in PIT was blown up in flames. LES BRIQUES was also fired on, obtaining 4 direct hits on building. Hits were also fired on enemy trench junction at A.28.c. 98. 92 (N. of CORONS DE MAROC.) Extent of damage could not be ascertained. X/46 Battery engaged several active trench mortars around HULLUCH. Y/46 Battery also engaged enemy trench mortars with good results between QUARRIES and CITÉ ST. ELIE. Z/46 Battery did considerable damage to enemy trenches and enemy trench mortars and also carried out a destructive shoot on enemy trench mortar at A.28.d. 18. 25 (near CORONS DE MAROC.) 2/Lieut Allen R.F.A 46 D.T.M. joined Trench Mortar Batteries & was attached to V/46 Battery. Casualties NIL.	
do.	18/12/17		V/46 Battery carried out a shoot against concrete emplacement at H.13.d. 45. 53 (HULLUCH) th request of Infantry who hit gas is installed at PITS 13. V/46 Battery obtained 3 direct hits on PIT, and blew up an ammunition dump. Considerable damage was also caused to LES BRIQUES. X/46 and Y/46 Batteries engaged and silenced several active hostile trench mortars	

Army Form C. 2118.

WAR DIARY
or
INTELLIGENCE SUMMARY.

46th Division Heavy and Medium Trench Mortar Batteries.

(Erase heading not required.)

Instructions regarding War Diaries and Intelligence Summaries are contained in F.S. Regs., Part II. and the Staff Manual respectively. Title pages will be prepared in manuscript.

Place	Date	Hour	Summary of Events and Information	Remarks and references to Appendices
Sailly Labourse	18/12/17 contd.		Z/46 Battery carried out a destructive shoot on several trench junctions around CORONS DE MAROC. 2/Lieut H.N. Cain R.F.A. proceeded on leave. Lieut. G.P. Clay admitted to hospital sick. # Lieut. E.E. Walker V/46 Battery took over the command of V/46 Battery. Casualties Nil.	
do.	19/12/17		V/46 Battery engaged enemy dump and sundry works in HULLUCH. Two small dumps were blown up and a concrete emplacement destroyed. Also carried out a destructive shoot on enemy trench junction at A28.d.23.78. (S. of LES BRIQUES). X/46 Battery engaged enemy artified shell holes N. of BOIS HUGO and enemy dug outs to the left of them. Direct hits were obtained on targets doing very considerable damage. Y/46 Battery carried out a destructive shoot on enemy T.Ms. around the QUARRIES. Z/46 Battery carried out a destructive shoot on enemy trenches N. of CORONS DE MAROC. 6 R.F. inspected trench mortars in Cambrin Sector. 2/Lieut C. Liddi returned from leave & relieved 2/Lieut. E.L. Hollies of the command of Z/46 Battery. Casualties. Nil.	
do.	20/12/17		V/46 Battery carried out harassing fire on HULLUCH. Observation was impossible owing to mist. Y/46 and Z/46 Batteries carried out harassing fire on enemy trench mortars posts and trenches around QUARRIES and LES BRIQUES. Capt. N. Giblin returned from leave and resumed command of V/46 Battery. 2/Lieut. E.L. Hollies proceeded on leave. Casualties Nil.	

Army Form C. 2118.

WAR DIARY
or
INTELLIGENCE SUMMARY.
(Erase heading not required.)

46th Division Heavy and Medium Trench Mortar Batteries

Place	Date	Hour	Summary of Events and Information	Remarks and references to Appendices
Sailly Labourse	21/12/17		Average daily expenditure of ammunition for week ending June 21/12/17 - 33 rds. Heavy, and 158 rds. Medium weighing approximately 42 tons 8 cwts. V/46 Battery fired 15 rounds at PITS 13 obtaining 5 direct hits on PIT and causing enemy to retaliate. 14 rounds were also fired at LES BRIQUES obtaining several direct hits. Y/46 Battery 41 rounds at enemy T.M. and "pooh" around the QUARRIES. Z/46 Battery engaged and silenced enemy MINENWERFER at approx. A28.c.85.95. (Left of CORONS DE PEKIN), and also damaged enemy trench W. of LES BRIQUES. Casualties. NIL.	
do.	22/12/17		V/46 Battery engaged enemy trench mortars around CITE ST. ELIE, and one emplacement was completely destroyed. Pits 13 was also engaged at request of Infantry and two direct hits obtained. Trench Mortar emplacement South of HULLUCH were engaged and direct hits obtained. One round was observed on to parapet, most probably a German. A destructive shoot was carried out on trench mortars and trench junctions around LES BRIQUES. X/46 Battery fired on trench mortar N. of BOIS HUGO and also considerably damaged enemy trench about H13c.78.28 (W. of HULLUCH) Y/46 Trench Mortar Battery carried out a destructive shoot on enemy post at G.12.a.40.03. (QUARRIES), but owing to a breakdown firing had to be discontinued. Z/46 Battery engaged enemy trench around LES BRIQUES and trench mortars, considerable damage being done. Casualties :- 6 ORs (V/46 Battery) wounded by enemy shell gas, but remained at duty.	

WAR DIARY or INTELLIGENCE SUMMARY

Army Form C. 2118.

46th Division Heavy and Medium Trench Mortar Batteries

Place	Date	Hour	Summary of Events and Information	Remarks and references to Appendices
Sailly Labourse	23/12/17		1/46 Battery considerably damaged enemy trench (CHATEAU ALLEY)(W. of AUCHY-LEZ-LA BASSÉE). Enemy dump in HULLUCH was engaged and a considerable amount of debris was thrown up. Two rounds caused unusually dense clouds of smoke and enemy retaliated on our trenches between CITE ST ELIE and HULLUCH. In active enemy T.M. in HULLUCH was engaged and 2 direct hits obtained on spot where flashes were seen. 15 rds were fired on enemy T.M's and PUITS 13. Rails in rear & left of PUITS known into the air. Enemy retaliated on our front line trench. x/46 Battery engaged enemy T.M. and trenches N. of BOIS HUGO and obtained several direct hits. New work seen in HULLUCH was fired on and was very much knocked about. Z/46 Battery engaged enemy "nook" in QUARRIES. Z/46 Battery fired on several enemy trenches doing considerable damage. Casualties. NIL.	
do.	24/12/17		1/46 Battery fired 10 rounds on enemy H.Q. in HULLUCH. Observation for effect impossible owing to mist. Trench Junction of HOBART and HOBBS ALLEY (N. of BOIS HUGO was engaged by x/46 Battery but visibility was too low to observe effect. Y/46 Battery cut several gaps in front of enemy front line between CITE ST ELIE and HULLUCH. Z/46 Battery engaged and silenced two enemy trench mortars around LESBRIQUES. A destructive shoot was also carried out on trench mortars and trenches in his vicinity. Casualties NIL.	

Army Form C. 2118.

WAR DIARY
INTELLIGENCE SUMMARY. 46th Division Heavy and Medium Trench Mortar Batteries.

(Erase heading not required.)

Place	Date	Hour	Summary of Events and Information	Remarks and references to Appendices
Sailly Labourse	25/12/17		Y/46 Battery engaged enemy H.Q. in HULLUCH. Target could not actually be seen but shooting was believed to be accurate. Buildings around HULLUCH Schoolhouse were also fired on and 6 explosions in quick succession were caused, in accordance with Ot Elie Group Order No. 23. PUITS 13 and T.Ms around CITÉ ST. ELIE were engaged. One T.M. emplacement was destroyed. X/46 Battery cut enemy wire and damaged enemy trenches N. of Bois HUGO. In accordance with St. Elie Group 0023 Y/46 Battery engaged enemy T.M. near CITÉ ST. ELIE. Casualties NIL.	
do.	26/12/17		Enemy "PILL BOX" at H132.30.50 was engaged by Y/46 and X/46 Batteries and much damage was done. 10 rounds were fired against enemy dug outs, trench mortars and machine guns in HAMLET trench (between CITE ST ELIE and HULLUCH.) Great damage was done. X/46 Battery engaged enemy dug outs and T.M. N.of BOIS HUGO. Several direct hits were obtained on T.M. and trenches were much blown about. Z/46 Battery fired 31 rounds on enemy trenches around CORONS DE MAROC, and much damage was caused. Average daily expenditure of trench mortar ammunition for week ending Jan. 28th:- Heavy 45 rounds, Medium - 130. Total weight equals 43 tons 10 cwts. Capt. E.R. Munro M.C. proceeded on leave equals 10 cwts. Capt. J.T.N.O Casualties NIL. Capt. A. Giblin took up the duties of J.T.M.O.	
do.	27/12/17		Y/46 Battery engaged and silenced enemy T.M. in HULLUCH at request of Infantry. X/46 Battery fired 35 rounds at M.G. emplacement in HULLUCH trench, also M.G. in HULLUCH. In accordance with Group Order Y/46 Battery engaged enemy trench mortar N. of QUARRIES. Casualties NIL. 2 ORs reported as being wounded and evacuated at duty on 22/12/17 now admitted to hospital suffering from effects of shell gas.	

Army Form C. 2118.

WAR DIARY
or
INTELLIGENCE SUMMARY.
(Erase heading not required.)

46th Division Heavy and Medium Trench Mortar Batteries

Place	Date	Hour	Summary of Events and Information	Remarks and references to Appendices
Sailly Labourse	28/12/17		Y/46 Battery fired on 2 enemy trench mortars west of LES BRIQUES. Much debris was blown up including a quantity of dugout timber. Enemy dug out in HAMLET TRENCH at concepts OP in CITE ST. ELIE were fired on. Eight rear corner of OP was knocked on. An enemy T.M. S.of HULLUCH and enemy OP in HULLUCH were engaged, and good shooting was made. X/46 Battery engaged enemy new work S.W. entrance of HULLUCH. 30 rounds fell on new work, and enemy retaliated on an new trench. Enemy trench mortar in HULLUCH were also fired on, and an enemy T.M. believed to be destroyed including a bomb store. Enemy retaliated and sent up a green light but no apparent action followed. Y/46 Battery carried out a destructive shoot on enemy T.M. between QUARRIES and CITE ST. ELIE. Z/46 Battery carried out a destructive shoot on enemy communication trenches around CORONS DE MAROC. Enemy heavily retaliated with trench mortars. Casualties NIL.	
do.	29/12/17		Y/46 Battery fired 15 rounds on TRAIN ALLEY (W. of LES BRIQUES). A great deal of debris was thrown up. Enemy retaliated with 4.2's. 11 rounds were fired at enemy T.M. in CITE ST. ELIE in accordance with Op. Elie Grap. 0.27. X/46 Battery engaged and silenced an enemy trench mortar on western outskirt of HULLUCH, and also engaged another trench mortar in same vicinity. Enemy retaliated with 4.2's. Y/46 Battery fired 60 rds in a destructive shoot on enemy trench mortar in CITE ST. ELIE, in accordance with Grap. 0.27. Casualties - NIL.	

Army Form C. 2118.

46th Division Heavy and
Medium Trench Mortar Btss.

WAR DIARY
or
INTELLIGENCE SUMMARY.
(Erase heading not required.)

Instructions regarding War Diaries and Intelligence Summaries are contained in F. S. Regs., Part II. and the Staff Manual respectively. Title pages will be prepared in manuscript.

Place	Date	Hour	Summary of Events and Information	Remarks and references to Appendices
Sailly Labourse	30/12/17		V/46 Battery fired 15 rounds on LES BRIQUES and AUCHY ALLEY. 2 direct hits were obtained on road, 2 in AUCHY ALLEY and 6 in LES BRIQUES. Smoke was observed to be coming from LES BRIQUES and a direct hit was obtained on it. An enemy T.M. in same vicinity was also fired on causing much debris to be thrown up. Enemy retaliated with 4.2s. 10 rounds were fired into HULLUCH. Observation was difficult owing to mist. Enemy retaliated on position. X/46 Battery fired 30 rounds on northern edge of HULLUCH, and a quantity of timber was thrown up. 30 rounds were fired at active T.M. south of HULLUCH and silenced. Enemy retaliated on CHALK PIT. Y/46 Battery engaged and silenced enemy T.M. in QUARRIES at request of Infantry. Z/46 Battery fired 30 rds at FOSSE Trench (near CORONS DE MAROC) Much timber was thrown up. Enemy TMS W. of LES BRIQUES were engaged but effect of fire could not be seen owing to mist. Enemy retaliated on position. Casualties Nil.	
do.	31/12/17		V/46 Battery fired on LES BRIQUES, and AUCHY ALLEY. 1 direct hit was obtained on road, 2 in AUCHY ALLEY and 6 in LES BRIQUES. In accordance with Corps order, enemy T.M. south of LES BRIQUES was engaged. Enemy retaliated on our trenches with 4.2s. X/46 Battery engaged enemy T.M. Nork of BOIS HUGO. A trench junction was destroyed and presumably an enemy T.M. and dug out. Trench Mortars in enemy second line trench (HULLUCH) and enemy dug out in third line were fired on. T.Ms were silenced and dug out blown up.	

A 5834 Wt. W4973/M687 730,000 8/16 D. D. & L. Ltd. Form/C.2113/13.

Army Form C. 2118.

WAR DIARY
or
INTELLIGENCE SUMMARY.

(Erase heading not required.)

46th Division Heavy and Medium Trench Mortar Batteries

Place	Date	Hour	Summary of Events and Information	Remarks and references to Appendices
Sailly Labourse	31/12/17 contd		Y/46 Battery engaged enemy T.M. Southern edge of CITE ST. ELIE, in retaliation acted for by Infantry. Z/46 Battery fired on enemy communications & dug outs around CORONS DE MAROC. Silent hits were also obtained on active enemy T.M. in same vicinity. Casualties Nil.	
			Total casualties during month of December 1917:- ORs.	
			V/46 Battery :- 5 wounded but remained at duty. 2 wounded & admitted to hospital.	
			X/46 Battery :- 1 OR wounded but remained at duty.	
			Y/46 Battery :- 2 ORs. wounded and admitted to hospital.	
			Z/46 Battery :- Nil.	
	2/1/18.			

Walker
Captain R.F.A.
O.T.M.O. 46th Division

CONFIDENTIAL.

WAR DIARY.

TRENCH MORTAR BATTERIES.

JANUARY 1st: to JANUARY 31st: 1918.

xxxxxxxx.xx

Army Form C. 2118.

WAR DIARY
or
INTELLIGENCE SUMMARY.
(Erase heading not required.)

46th Divisional Heavy and Medium Trench Mortar Batteries.

Place	Date	Hour	Summary of Events and Information	Remarks and references to Appendices
Sailly Labourse	1/1/18		Y/46 Battery engaged targets in HULLUCH and BENIFONTAINE and enemy dug outs, trench mortars, machine guns and dumps in HAMLET Trench (S. of CITÉ ST. ELIE.) Good deal of damage was caused. X/46 Battery engaged enemy machine gun and O.P. at H13d 30.50 (S. end of HULLUCH) and enemy dug outs and trench mortars at H26a 15.85 (N. of BOIS HUGO) doing considerable damage. Z/46 Battery fired on enemy trenches in CAMBRIN Sector. Much damage is believed to have been caused. G.O.C. inspected trench mortar positions in CAMBRIN Sector. Casualties NIL.	
do.	2/1/18		Y/46 and X/46 Batteries fired on enemy trenches and trench mortars around HULLUCH and LES BRIQUES. Explosions were caused in several places. Y/46 Battery engaged G.13a 85.30 (QUARRIES) in accordance with Pt. Élie Group O.29 and by special request of Infantry and also fired 10 rounds in reply to "S.O.S LANCER". Z/46 Battery obtained 7 direct hits on enemy trench mortar at A28d 23.75 (S. of LES BRIQUES). Casualties NIL.	
do.	3/1/18		Y/46 Battery engaged and silenced enemy trench mortars in CITÉ ST. ELIE and HULLUCH. X/46. Y/46. and Z/46 Batteries also engaged enemy trench mortars and trench junctions on their respective fronts. Explosions were caused at several places. Y/46 Battery commenced work on an alternative emplacement off STANSFIELD TUNNEL. Casualties NIL.	

WAR DIARY or INTELLIGENCE SUMMARY

Army Form C. 2118.

46th Divisional Heavy and Medium T.M. Batteries.

Place	Date	Hour	Summary of Events and Information	Remarks and references to Appendices
Sailly Labourse	4/1/18		Y/46 Battery fired on LES BRIQUES and enemy trenches in vicinity. Direct hits were obtained. Z/46 Battery fired on enemy trench mortars around LES BRIQUES in retaliation to enemy trench mortar fire. Y/46 Battery fired a 6 inch trench mortar in action in CLIFFORD STREET. Casualties:- 1 OR Z/46 Battery wounded and admitted to hospital.	
do.	5/1/18		Y/46 Battery engaged hostile trench mortars around LES BRIQUES. Visibility poor. Z/46 Battery fired on hostile trench mortars and enemy trench junction W. of LES BRIQUES. Casualties:- NIL. Z/46 Battery put a 6 inch mortar in action in MAISON ROUGE ALLEY.	
do.	6/1/18		Y/46 Battery engaged and silenced a hostile machine gun S. of CITÉ ST. ELIE at request of Infantry. Several enemy trench mortars were engaged and silenced. X/46 Battery engaged movement seen in HULLUCH. Z/46 Battery engaged an enemy trench mortar immediately S. of LES BRIQUES. A round appeared to drop down shaft of T.M. emplacement. Casualties NIL.	
do.	7/1/18		Y/46 Battery fired on an enemy trench mortar in CITÉ ST. ELIE obtaining several good hits. X/46 Battery fired on HULLUCH trench. Visibility was very poor. Y/46 Battery silenced enemy trench mortars and also registered the new mortar in CLIFFORD STREET. Casualties:- NIL.	
do.	8/1/18 and 9/1/18.		Y/46 Battery engaged several enemy machine guns south of CITÉ ST. ELIE. X/46 Battery engaged enemy wire S.W. of HULLUCH. Y/46 Battery engaged several enemy trench mortars between QUARRIES and CITÉ ST. ELIE. and	

Army Form C. 2118.

WAR DIARY
or
INTELLIGENCE SUMMARY
(Erase heading not required.)

46th Division Heavy and Medium Trench Mortar Batteries.

Instructions regarding War Diaries and Intelligence Summaries are contained in F.S. Regs., Part II. and the Staff Manual respectively. Title pages will be prepared in manuscript.

Place	Date	Hour	Summary of Events and Information	Remarks and references to Appendices
Sailly Labourse	9/1/18 contd.		Z/46 Battery registered a 6 inch mortar on LES BRIQUES, and engaged enemy trench mortars in retaliation. Casualties Nil.	
do.	10/1/18		X/46 Battery fired on an enemy trench mortar N. of BOIS HUGO causing much debris to be blown up. Z/46 Battery engaged enemy trench and trench mortar around LES BRIQUES. Several direct hits were obtained. Casualties Nil.	
do.	11/1/18		V/46 Battery engaged hostile trench mortars in a destructive shoot. X/46 Battery obtained several direct hits on T.M. position in HULLUCH. Y/46 Battery silenced a hostile T.M. between QUARRIES and CITÉ ST ELIE. Z/46 Battery engaged two enemy trench junction but observation was difficult owing to mist. Casualties - Nil. Capt. N. Gillis resumed command of Y/46 Bty. vice Capt. C. Mawr M.C. returned from leave.	
do.	12/1/18		V/46 Battery carried out several destructive shoots on enemy trench mortars around HULLUCH, and also silenced active ones at request of Infantry. X/46 Battery also co-operated with the above. Z/46 Battery carried out a destructive shoot on enemy front line W. of LES BRIQUES. Casualties - Nil.	
do.	13/1/18		V/46 Battery engaged an enemy trench mortar in HULLUCH at request of Infantry. Much damage was caused. X/46 and Y/46 Batteries carried out destructive shoots on enemy trench mortars. Casualties - Nil. V/46 - Z/46 Battery carried out a destructive shoot on enemy trench mortar in CITÉ ST ELIE and HULLUCH. Y/46 and Z/46 Batteries carried out destructive shoot.	
do.	14/1/18			

WAR DIARY

Army Form C. 2118.

of 46th Division Heavy and Medium Trench Mortar Batteries.

INTELLIGENCE SUMMARY.

(Erase heading not required.)

Place	Date	Hour	Summary of Events and Information	Remarks and references to Appendices
Sailly Labourse	14/1/18		On enemy trenches. O.R.A. inspected trench mortar positions in CAMBRIN SECTOR. Casualties - NIL.	
do.	15/1/18 contd.		Y/46 Battery engaged enemy trench mortar at A28a.95.88 (W. of LES BRIQUES) in a destructive shoot and also fired on tunnel entrance at S.E. edge of HULLUCH. Owing to mist effect of fire could not be seen. X/46 Battery engaged a trench mortar in HULLUCH in a destructive shoot and a fire was caused. Z/46 Battery put one 6 inch mortar in action in BARTS ALLEY. D.T.M.O. 11th Division and Battery Officers visited us and inspected billets etc. and arranged relief of Batteries. Casualties - NIL.	
do.	16/1/18		Y/46 Battery fired on Company H.Q. and enemy trench mortar in CITE ST.ELIE. Trench Aerio was thrown up. Y/46 and Z/46 Batteries engaged several trench mortars. X/46 Battery put a 6 inch mortar in action of ST.ELIE tunnel. Casualties - NIL.	
do.	17/1/18		Y/46 Battery engaged and silenced active enemy trench mortar in HULLUCH. Z/46 Battery fired 20 rounds into AUCHY ALLEY, but owing to mist, damage caused could not be observed. O.R.A. inspected new 6 inch trench mortar positions on ST.ELIE SECTOR. Casualties - NIL.	
do.	18/1/18		Y/46 Battery fired 15 rds at enemy trench mortar in second line trench South of CITE ST.ELIE. Corrugated iron and timber was thrown up and hand grenades were exploded. X/46 and Y/46 Batteries engaged and silenced	

WAR DIARY

INTELLIGENCE SUMMARY.

Army Form C. 2118.

46th Division Heavy and Medium Trench Mortar Batteries

Place	Date	Hour	Summary of Events and Information	Remarks and references to Appendices
Sailly Labourse	18/1/18 Contd.		Casualties – NIL.	
	19/1/18		Y/46 Battery fired 26 rounds on tunnel entrance S.E. corner of HULLUCH and 10 rds on enemy tram line near LES BRIQUES. Two direct hits were obtained on tunnel entrance and one on tram line. Y/46 Battery carried out a shoot with aeroplane observation on 2 enemy trench mortars and direct hits were obtained. Lieut Knox proceeded on 14 days leave to England. Casualties – NIL.	
do.	20/1/18		Y/46 Battery fired 10 rds in a destructive shoot on enemy trench mortar near LES BRIQUES. 2/Lieut. G.P. Clay returned from Hospital and resumed command of Y/46 Battery. Casualties – NIL.	
do.	21/1/18		Y/46 Battery engaged an enemy trench mortar at H.7.a.22.40 (midway between CITÉ ST ELIE and HULLUCH) and obtained a direct hit and fired 10 rounds at enemy machine gun near LES BRIQUES which caused an explosion causing dense black smoke to rise. Z/46 Battery fired on enemy dump at FOSSE 8 and a small fire was caused. Two direct hits were also obtained on AUCHY ALLEY. Lieut. E. Balme admitted to Hospital sick. 2/Lieut. E. Allen returned from leave. Casualties – NIL.	
do.	22/1/18		Y/46 Battery obtained 2 direct hits on enemy trench mortar in HULLUCH. Z/46 Battery caused considerable damage to enemy trenches and trench mortar emplacements around CORONS DE MAROC. Casualties – NIL.	

WAR DIARY
or
INTELLIGENCE SUMMARY

Army Form C. 2118.

46th Division Heavy and Medium Trench Mortar Batteries.

Place	Date	Hour	Summary of Events and Information	Remarks and references to Appendices
Sailly Labourse	23/1/18		V/46 Battery fired Rnds at enemy trench mortar N. of BOIS HUGO. Direct hits on tunnel entrance and enemy trench were obtained. The enemy trench mortar first S. of LES BRIQUES was also engaged and direct hits obtained. Z/46 Battery carried out a destructive shoot on AUCHY ALLEY. Advanced party of 11th Div. H.y. Trench Mortar Battery (4 Officers and 12 ORs) arrived to reconnoitre line. 2/Lt. B.E.V. Wildman proceeded on leave. Casualties – Nil.	
do.	24/1/18		Firing – Nil. 11th Div. H.y. Trench Mortar Battery arrived to take over. 2/Lt. E.H. Wicks returned from leave. Casualties – Nil.	
do.	25/1/18		Batteries in the line relieved by Batteries of 11th Div. H.y. T.M. Bty. All guns were handed over. Relief was completed by 4.0pm except for one Officer per Battery who remained with new Batteries until 9.0am. Lieut. E.P. Islay proceeded to First Army Trench Mortar School as Instructor. Casualties – Nil.	
do.	26/1/18		Batteries marched into Billets at VENDIN-LEZ-BETHUNE. D.T.M.O's office moved with HQRs. to GONNEHEM. Casualties – Nil.	
Gonnehem	27/1/18		Batteries commenced a period of training. Casualties – Nil.	

WAR DIARY
or
INTELLIGENCE SUMMARY.

46th Division Heavy and Medium Trench Mortar Batteries

Army Form C. 2118.

Place	Date	Hour	Summary of Events and Information	Remarks and references to Appendices
Gonnelieu	28/1/18		Orders received re-organization of Trench Mortar Batteries and the formation of a Corps Heavy Trench Mortar Battery. It is proposed to form two such Trench Mortar Batteries per Division. The Corps Heavy Trench Mortar Battery being detached from a Division and administered by Corps. Total Casualties during month of January :— 1 O.R. wounded.	

A.D.Munro
Captain R.F.A.
D.T.M.O. 46th Division.

CONFIDENTIAL.

WAR DIARY.

TRENCH MORTAR BATTERIES.

FEBRUARY 1st: to FEBRUARY 28th: 1918.

xxxxxxx

Army Form C. 2118.

kms
46th Division Medium Trench
Mortar Batteries.

Vol 24

WAR DIARY
or
INTELLIGENCE SUMMARY.
(Erase heading not required.)

Place	Date	Hour	Summary of Events and Information	Remarks and references to Appendices
Gonnehem	1/2/18		Trench Mortar Batteries commenced a schedule of training drawn up by Divisional Trench Mortar Officer. First day :- Smoke Helmet drill, Marching drill with arms, Signalling. Casualties :- Nil.	
do.	2/2/18		Second day :- Squad drill with arms, Marching drill. Casualties :- Nil.	
do.	3/2/18		Third day :- 4 Officers and 40 ORs proceeded on a course in 6 inch Trench Mortars at Army Trench Mortar School. 2/Lieut. H. N. Cain and 26 ORs of V/46 Trench Mortar Battery left 46th Division and joined 160th Heavy Trench Mortar Battery. Remaining Officers and ORs of V/46 Trench Mortar Battery posted to X/46 and Y/46 Trench Mortar Batteries to complete establishment. Z/46 Trench Mortar Battery disbanded and officers and personnel distributed between X/46 and Y/46 Trench Mortar Batteries. Division now has two Medium Trench Mortar Batteries viz :- X/46 and Y/46, consisting of 4 Officers and 52 ORs per Battery, each Battery manning 6 guns. Trench Mortar Batteries carried out firing practice on Rifle Ranges at ANNEZIN FOSSE (E.7.b.) Casualties :- Nil.	
do.	4/2/18		Fourth day :- Physical drill, Route March, Signalling. Men reading. Lieut. E. N. Snoch returned from leave, and proceeded to Army Trench Mortar	

Army Form C. 2118.

WAR DIARY
or
INTELLIGENCE SUMMARY.

(Erase heading not required.)

46th Division Medium Trench Mortar Battery.

Instructions regarding War Diaries and Intelligence Summaries are contained in F.S. Regs., Part II. and the Staff Manual respectively. Title pages will be prepared in manuscript.

Place	Date	Hour	Summary of Events and Information	Remarks and references to Appendices
Gonnehem	4/2/18 contd		School for a course on Trench Mortar. Casualties:- Nil.	
do.	5/2/18		Fifth day:- Physical drill, Squad drill with arms. Marching drill, Signalling. Casualties:- Nil.	
do.	6/2/18		Sixth day:- Exercise. Physical training, Squad drill with arms. Marching drill. Casualties:- Nil.	
do.	7/2/18		Seventh day:- Exercises. Route March. Casualties:- Nil.	
do.	8/2/18		Eighth day:- Exercises. Squad drill with arms. Marching drill. Signalling and Map reading. Casualties:- Nil.	
do.	9/2/18		Exercises. Physical training. Preparations for move. 2 Lt. 367. Wildman returned from leave. Casualties:- Nil.	
do.	10/2/18		Tenth day:- Battery marched with 46th Divisional Ammunition Column to Bomy Area, arriving at Bellebrune on 11th.	
do.	11/2/18		Tenth day:- Officer moved with Headquarters R.F.A. to Verchin.	
do.	12/2/18		Chateau. 4 Officers and 41 ORs returned from camp at Army School.	
Verchin	13/2/18		4 Officers and 87 ORs proceeded on a course at Army Rest. Nil.	
do.	15/2/18		Fifteenth day:- Battery moved from Bellebrune to Crepy. Casualties:- Nil.	

WAR DIARY
or
INTELLIGENCE SUMMARY

40th Division Medium Trench Mortar Batteries.

Army Form C. 2118.

(Erase heading not required.)

Place	Date	Hour	Summary of Events and Information	Remarks and references to Appendices
Verchin	14/2/18		Fourteenth day:- Exercises and Physical drill. Squad and rifle drill. Musketry. Signalling. Map reading. 2/Lieut. J.W. Edge proceeded on 14 days leave to England. Casualties:- Nil.	
do.	15/2/18		Sixteenth day:- Physical drill. Rifle and Marching drill. Casualties:- Nil.	
do.	17/2/18		Seventeenth day:- Physical drill. Kit inspection. Casualties:- Nil.	
do.	18/2/18		Eighteenth day:- Exercises. Inspection Parade. Route March in Marching Order. Musketry. Signalling. Casualties:- Nil.	
do.	19/2/18		Nineteenth day:- Exercises Inspection parade. Scabies inspection. Physical training. Rifle and Marching drill. Map reading. Signalling. 15 ORs returned from First Army School of Mines. 2/Lieut B.E.T. Wildman left Trench Mortar Batteries and joined 6th Nth Staffs Regt. Casualties:- Nil.	
do.	20/2/18		Twentieth day:- Exercises. Inspection parade. Bathing parade. Brigade Marching drill. Musketry. Signalling. 8 ORs Proceeded on a course at First Army School of Mines. Casualties:- Nil.	
do.	21/2/18		Twenty first day:- Exercises. Inspection parade. Route March. Map reading. Signalling. Lecture. Casualties:- Nil.	
do.	22/2/18		Twenty second day:- Exercises. Inspection parade. Physical training. Brigade Marching drill. Anti-gas drill. Musketry. Signalling. Casualties:- Nil.	

WAR DIARY or INTELLIGENCE SUMMARY

Army Form C. 2118.

46th Division Medium Trench Mortar Batteries.

(Erase heading not required.)

Instructions regarding War Diaries and Intelligence Summaries are contained in F. S. Regs., Part II. and the Staff Manual respectively. Title pages will be prepared in manuscript.

Place	Date	Hour	Summary of Events and Information	Remarks and references to Appendices
Verchin	23/2/18		Twenty third day :- Exercises, Inspection Parade, Physical training, Rifle and Marching drill. Casualties :- NIL.	
do.	24/2/18		Twenty fourth day :- Exercises, Inspection Parade, Church Parade. Afternoon: Half Holiday. Casualties :- NIL.	
do.	25/2/18		Twenty fifth day :- Exercises, Inspection Parade, Route March in full marching order, Nonohely. Lecture. Casualties :- NIL.	
do.	26/2/18		Twenty sixth day :- 2/Lieut. B. Tolls admitted to hospital sick. Battery marched at 9.15am from Verchin to Allouagne to join 46th Division Training Battalion, arriving at destination at 4.0pm. Casualties :- NIL.	
Allouagne	27/2/18		Training under 46th Div Training Battalion.	
"	28/2/18		" " " " "	

McManus Capt. RFA
DTMO 46th D.A.

CONFIDENTIAL.

WAR DIARY.

TRENCH MORTAR BATTERIES.

MARCH 1st: to MARCH 31st: 1918.

WAR DIARY
INTELLIGENCE SUMMARY

Army Form C. 2118.

46th Division Medium Trench Mortar Batteries.

VOL 25

Place	Date	Hour	Summary of Events and Information	Remarks and references to Appendices
Techin	1/3/18		Training of Batteries at 46th Div. Training Battalion continued. – Casualties – NIL.	
do.	2/3/18		2/Lieut. J. W. Edge rejoined from leave. Casualties – NIL.	
do.	3rd 4/3/18		Training continued at Div. Training Battalion. Casualties – NIL.	
do.	5/3/18		Headquarters of D.T.M.O. moved with Headquarters R.A. from Techin to Fouquières. D.T.M.O. and O.C. X/46 Trench Mortar Battery reconnoitred positions in the line in preparation to taking over from 11th Division. Y/46 Trench Mortar Battery marched from Allouagne to Lillers. in Annequin. Casualties – NIL.	
Fouquières.	6/3/18		D.T.M.O. and O.C. X/46 Trench Mortar Battery reconnoitred positions in the line to be taken over from 55th Division. Y/46 Trench Mortar Battery relieved one medium Trench Mortar Battery of 11th Division on Cambrin and Hohenzollern Sectors. X/46 Trench Mortar Battery marched from Allouagne to Lillers in Annequin. Casualties – NIL.	
do.	7/3/18		X/46 Trench Mortar Battery relieved one medium Battery of 55th Division in Cuinchy Sector. 2/Lieut. E. Porter joined Y/46 Trench Mortar Battery from 46th Divisional Ammunition Column. Casualties – NIL.	
Annequin	8/3/18		Headquarters of D.T.M.O. moved from Fouquières to Annequin. Y/46 Trench Mortar Battery fired 12 rounds in neutralisation of enemy trench mortars. Casualties – NIL.	

Army Form C. 2118.

WAR DIARY

INTELLIGENCE SUMMARY.
(Erase heading not required.)

46th Division Medium Trench Mortar Battery.

Place	Date	Hour	Summary of Events and Information	Remarks and references to Appendices
Annequin	9/3/18.		40 rds were fired in silencing enemy trench mortars during the day. Casualties - Nil.	
do.	10/3/18.		25 rds T.M.F. fired by X/46 Trench Mortar Battery in verification of target handed over by 55th Division. Y/46 Trench Mortar Battery fired 14 rds. in neutralisation of enemy trench mortars. Casualties - Nil.	
do.	11/3/18.		X/46 Trench Mortar Battery fired 21 rds in silencing enemy trench mortars. Y/46 Trench Mortar Battery fired 37 rds in silencing trench mortars. Casualties - Nil.	
do.	12/3/18.		X/46 Trench Mortar Battery fired 15 rds in silencing enemy mortars. Y/46 Trench Mortar Battery obtained 10 direct hits on an active hostile mortar reported by Infantry. 57 rds were also fired in neutralising enemy mortars. 2/Lieut. T.F. Bromwell joined X/46 Battery from 231st Brigade R.F.A. 2/Lieut. J.F. Nash joined Y/46 Battery from 46th Divisional Ammunition Column. Casualties - Nil.	
do.	13/3/18		X/46 Battery fired 40 rds in neutralising enemy mortars. Y/46 Battery fired 48 rds in neutralisation. 2/Lieut. F.L.F. Morrison joined Y/46 Battery from 230th Brigade R.F.A. Casualties - Nil.	
do.	14/3/18		Y/46 Battery fired 46 rds in neutralisation. Casualties - Nil.	
do.	15/3/18		32 rounds fired by X/46 and Y/46 Batteries in neutralisation. 8 rds fired on enemy working party which was successfully dispersed. Casualties - Nil.	

WAR DIARY
INTELLIGENCE SUMMARY

Army Form C. 2118.

46th Division Medium Trench Mortar Batteries.

Place	Date	Hour	Summary of Events and Information	Remarks and references to Appendices
Annequin	16/3/18		X/46 Battery fired 55 rds at enemy wire doing considerable damage, and blowing up an ammunition dump. Y/46 Battery fired 18 rounds in neutralisation and 22 rds in registration and obtaining working parties. Casualties - Nil.	
do.	17/3/18		X/46 Battery fired 10 rds in neutralising enemy mortars in conjunction with a raid by left Division. Y/46 Battery fired 17 rds in neutralisation. Casualties - Nil.	
do.	18/3/18		Y/46 Battery fired 6 rds in neutralisation. Casualties - Nil.	
do.	19/3/18		X/46 Battery fired 20 rds in neutralising enemy trench mortars by order of Corps. Y/46 Battery fired 25 rds in neutralisation. Several direct hits were obtained on an enemy sniping post. Sandbags and sniping shield were blown up. Casualties :- 2/Lt. A.J.F. Thompson, Y/46 Battery wounded by H.E. but remained at duty.	
do.	20/3/18		12 rds fired in neutralisation of enemy trench mortars. 2/Lieut. C. Tidey proceeded on 14 days leave to England. Casualties - Nil.	
do.	21/3/18		Y/46 Battery silenced an enemy trench mortar at request of Infantry. Casualties - Nil.	
do.	22/3/18		X/46 Battery fired 33 rds on an enemy trench (MILL ALLEY.) Enemy retaliated with 4.2s on our position, obtaining one direct hit on No. 4 gun. During enemy raid on night of 21st/22nd, Y/46 Battery fired 96 rds on S.O.S. target; and during the morning 15 rds in neutralising enemy trench mortars. Casualties - Nil.	
do.	23/3/18		6 rds fired in neutralisation. Casualties - Nil.	

WAR DIARY

INTELLIGENCE SUMMARY

Army Form C. 2118.

46th Division Medium Trench Mortar Batteries.

Place	Date	Hour	Summary of Events and Information	Remarks and references to Appendices
Annequin	24/3/18		X/46 Battery fired 20 rds in neutralising enemy trench mortars. Y/46 Battery fired 15 rds in registering an enemy trench mortar and obtained 3 direct hits. Casualties – NIL.	
do.	25/3/18		X/46 Battery fired 10 rds in neutralisation. 2/Lt. J.T. Nash rejoined X/46 Battery from 46th Divisional Ammunition Column. 2/Lt. J.E. Gillespie joined Y/46 Trench Mortar Battery from 46th Divisional Ammunition Column. Casualties – NIL.	
do.	26/3/18		X/46 Battery fired 39 rds in registration of S.O.S. lines. Y/46 Trench Mortar Battery fired 30 rds in a destructive shoot on an enemy trench mortar. Left emplacement of enemy position destroyed and whole area around position plowed up. 2 rounds fell in left emplacement and 4 rounds were reported O.K. 20 rounds were also fired in a destructive shoot on another enemy mortar. 6 direct hits were obtained and remainder fell all around target. Casualties – NIL.	
do.	27/3/18		X/46 Battery fired 15 rounds in neutralisation. Y/46 Battery fired 29 rounds in neutralisation of enemy trench mortar. 9 rds were fired on AUCHY ALLEY and 6 direct hits were obtained. Lieut. G.P. Clay rejoined from First Army School of Mortars. Casualties – NIL.	
do.	28/3/18		Y/46 Battery relieved in action by one medium Trench Mortar Battery of 11th Division in Cambrin and Hohenzollern Sectors, and then marched to Beuvry & Cité St. Emile Sectors and relieved 4th Canadian Trench Mortar Batteries.	

Army Form C. 2118.

46th Division Medium
Trench Mortar Batteries.

WAR DIARY
or
INTELLIGENCE SUMMARY
(Erase heading not required.)

Place	Date	Hour	Summary of Events and Information	Remarks and references to Appendices
Annequin	28/3/18		X/46 Battery relieved in action by one medium Trench Mortar Battery of 55th Division in Cuinchy Sector, and then marched to Hill 70 Sector and relieved in action 5th Canadian Trench Mortar Batteries. Trench Mortar Headquarters moved to billets in Leo Brebis. Casualties = Nil.	
Leo Brebis	29/3/18		Casualties 10R (X/46 Battery) accidentally injured and admitted to hospital. Firing - Nil.	
do.	30/3/18		Firing - Nil. Casualties Nil	
do.	31/3/18		Firing - Nil. Casualties Nil	

DRMmm
Captain R.F.A.
D.T.M.O. 46th Divisional Arty.

46th Divisional Artillery.

46th DIVISIONAL TRENCH MORTARS

APRIL 1918.

WAR DIARY
or
INTELLIGENCE SUMMARY

Army Form C. 2118.

H.Q. Divisional Artillery Trench Mortar Batteries.

Vol 26

Place	Date	Hour	Summary of Events and Information	Remarks and references to Appendices
Field	2/4/18		X/46, 2.M.B. fired 26 Rds and Y/46 Dn.B. 25 Rds in retaliation to Enemy Trench Mortar fire. 8 Affects Z rocks.	
	3/4/18		No 820 517. Lieu Bennett J. X/Bty wounded admitted to hospital. X/Bty fired 67 Rounds and Y/Bty 17 Rounds in retaliation to enemy fire.	
	4/4/18		D.T.M.O. H.Q. and Batteries moved to billets in CITÉ St PIERRE near HQ. remained at LES BREBIS	
	5/4/18		8.20.600. Lieu Harriman A. wounded admitted to hospital. Y/1M.B. X/Battery fired 50 Rounds in retaliation to Enemy fire. 2nd Lt Rister attached 1st Corps signals in protection. X/Battery fired 20 Rounds and Y/Bty 45 in retaliation.	
	6/4/18		2nd Rust Covente admitted to hospital Issued (shell.) X/Battery fired 32 rounds Y/Bty 28 rounds in retaliation	
	7/4/18		X/Battery fired 38 rounds Y/Bty 39 rounds in retaliation	

Army Form C. 2118.

WAR DIARY
or
INTELLIGENCE SUMMARY.
(Erase heading not required.)

Place	Date	Hour	Summary of Events and Information	Remarks and references to Appendices
Field	8/4/18		"1 - 6" Land Howitzer Bed at Rear H.Q. destroyed by enemy shell fire.	
	9/4/18		Y/ Bty fired 19 Rounds in retaliation to enemy shelling	
	10/4/18		Construction of 14 Reserve positions commenced in charge of Lt. G. P. Clay	
	11/4/18		Nothing to report	
			Nothing to report	
	12/4/18		Relieved by 3rd Canadian Division Trench Mortar Batteries.	
	13/4/18		T.M.B.H.Q. and Batteries marched to Billets in MAISNIL-LE-RUITZ	
			Nothing to report	
	14/4/18		do	
	15/4/18		Commenced training	
	16/4/18		do	
	17/4/18		do	
	18/4/18		do	
	19/4/18		do	
	20/4/18		do	
	22/4/18		do	
	23/4/18		do	

Army Form C. 2118.

WAR DIARY
or
INTELLIGENCE SUMMARY.
(Erase heading not required.)

Instructions regarding War Diaries and Intelligence Summaries are contained in F. S. Regs., Part II. and the Staff Manual respectively. Title pages will be prepared in manuscript.

Place	Date	Hour	Summary of Events and Information	Remarks and references to Appendices
Fiefs	24/4/18		T.M.H.Q and B Batteries marched to billets at GOSNAY.	
	25/4/18		2nd Lt. B. L. Wilkes posted Y/46. I.Br.B. Auth AQ/2/57/777.Q 25/4/18.	
	26/4/18		Lieut. E. Allen returned to D A C for duty. 2/Lieut. Ly Gillespie joined Y/46. D. Br. B.	
	27/4/18		T.M.H.Q and B Batteries moved to new billets BETHUNE. New positions marked out.	
	28/4/18		Work commenced on new positions X/By 3 positions Y/By 4 positions.	
	29/4/18		Continued work on new positions.	
	30/4/18		T.M.H.Q moved to Billets on E side Bethune Canal. Work continued on new positions in Dock area by X/Batty. 2 positions completed.	

Aubrey Rawlins
Captain A.E. (?)
J. J. M. O. 46th Div. Arty

CONFIDENTIAL.

WAR DIARY.

TRENCH MORTAR BATTERIES.

May 1st: to May 31st: 1918.

Army Form C. 2118.

WAR DIARY
or
INTELLIGENCE SUMMARY.
(Erase heading not required.)

461. Bde. J. M. Batters   Vol 27

Instructions regarding War Diaries and Intelligence Summaries are contained in F.S. Regs., Part II. and the Staff Manual respectively. Title pages will be prepared in manuscript.

Place	Date	Hour	Summary of Events and Information	Remarks and references to Appendices
John hill	1st		J.M. Headquarters heavily shelled with gas shells. 9 officers and 63 O.R. admitted hospital (gassed)	
	3rd		Lieut (A/Capt) R.L. Hunter and Lieut J.W. Hewitt joined "Y" Battery.	
			26 ORs joined from 1st Army Reinforcement Camp.	
	4th		Bdr Potts wounded.	
	5th		1 OR admitted to hospital sick.	
	6th		Capt. C.A. Coulden joined as D.T.M.O. 3 ORs joined from 16th Division.	
			2 ORs admitted to hospital sick	
			1 OR admitted to hospital wounded.	
	7th		2 ORs returned to duty from hospital.	
	8th		Bdr. J. Key returned from gas course.	
			15 ORs posted from 461. D.A.C.	
			Lieut D.J. Strachan joined from 461 D.A.C.	
	9th		4 ORs admitted to hospital sick	
	10th		1 OR admitted to hospital sick	
	12th		7 guns in action	

Army Form C. 2118.

WAR DIARY
or
INTELLIGENCE SUMMARY.
(Erase heading not required.)

Instructions regarding War Diaries and Intelligence Summaries are contained in F. S. Regs., Part II. and the Staff Manual respectively. Title pages will be prepared in manuscript.

Place	Date	Hour	Summary of Events and Information	Remarks and references to Appendices
In the field	13th		2 OR Father C. promoted to Corporal. 1 OR admitted to hospital sick.	
	14th		Lieut. J. Thorion Orand joined from 14th Division. Lieut. G. P. Mitchfield and 1 OR joined from 14th Division. Received 300 rounds T.M.G. 9 guns in action.	
	15th		2 OR admitted to hospital sick. Received 100 rounds T.M.G. 9 guns in action.	
	16th		1 gun out of action through hostile M.G. fire. 9 guns in action. 1 OR returned to duty from hospital. 9 guns in action.	
	17th		1 Officer admitted to hospital sick. 2 OR Morris promoted to Corporal. 9 guns in action.	
	18th		Sgt. J.B. Kimble joined "Y" Battery. 1 OR returned to duty from hospital. 9 guns in action.	

Army Form C. 2118.

WAR DIARY
or
INTELLIGENCE SUMMARY.
(Erase heading not required.)

Instructions regarding War Diaries and Intelligence Summaries are contained in F. S. Regs., Part II. and the Staff Manual respectively. Title pages will be prepared in manuscript.

Place	Date	Hour	Summary of Events and Information	Remarks and references to Appendices
In the field	19th		"X" Battery fired 16 rounds on enemy wire.	
			1 Officer attached from 231 Bde. and 1 Officer attached from 250 Bde. R.F.A.	
			9 guns in action	
	20th		1 gun destroyed by shell fire. 10 guns in action.	
	21st		1 Officer and 2 ORs admitted phosphene sick.	
			1 gun received from D.A.D.O.S. H.bk. Div. 10 guns in action	
	22nd		7 ORs admitted to hospital sick.	
			Cpl Larkins J. awarded M.M.	
			Gnr Bean J. awarded M.M. authy. VII Corps No. G/134/556. d - 10.5.18.	
			10 guns in action.	
	23rd		10 ORs posted from 461 D.A.C. 10 guns in action	
	24th		10 guns in action	
	25th		2 Officers and 8 ORs to 1st Army School of Mortars for M.T.M. Course.	
			Gnr Berry died of wounds. 10 guns in action.	

Army Form C. 2118.

WAR DIARY
or
INTELLIGENCE SUMMARY.
(Erase heading not required.)

Instructions regarding War Diaries and Intelligence Summaries are contained in F. S. Regs., Part II. and the Staff Manual respectively. Title pages will be prepared in manuscript.

Place	Date	Hour	Summary of Events and Information	Remarks and references to Appendices
In the field	26th		Lieut. E. J. H. Butler joined from 231 Bde R.F.A. Lieut. J. M. Abele joined from 280 Bde R.F.A. 10 guns in action.	
	27th		"Y" Battery fired 20 rounds on X.23.a. 75.75. 10 guns in action.	
	28th		1 O.R. returned to duty from hospital on completion of duty. 3 Sub have received from R.E.s. 10 guns in action	
	29th		11 O.R. posted from 46th D.A.C. 4 Sub has received from D.A.D.O.S. 46th Div. 10 guns in action	
	30th		"Y" Battery fired 11 rounds in answer to S.O.S. rockets. Sent up at 2.30 a.m. 10 guns in action.	
	31st		Gnr Hand J. promoted to Bdr. 10 guns in action.	

J. Williamson
for Capt.
46th D.T.M.O.

CONFIDENTIAL.

WAR DIARY.

TRENCH MORTAR BATTERIES.

JUNE 1st: 1918 to JUNE 30th: 1918.

Army Form C. 2118.

WAR DIARY
46th Dvn. T.M.B
or
INTELLIGENCE SUMMARY.
(Erase heading not required.)

JUNE 1918

Place	Date	Hour	Summary of Events and Information	Remarks and references to Appendices
In the field	1st		1 O.R. returned to duty from hospital. Received 200 rounds T.M.G.	
	2nd		Received 200 rounds T.M.G. 5 O.R. to 1st Corps R.A. Rest Camp. 10 guns in action.	
	3rd		10 guns in action.	
	4th		ditto.	
	5th		4 O.R's passed from 46th D.A.C. 6 sub fuses received from D.A.D.O.S. 46th Dn.	
			10 guns in action.	
	7th		Gunner Johnston L. granted 1 months re-engagement leave. 10 guns in action.	
	8th		5 sub fuses received from R.E's. 2 Officers and 8 O.R. returned from T.M. Course.	
			11 guns in action.	
	9th		5 O.R's returned from 1st Corps Rest Camp. 11 guns in action.	
	10th		11 guns in action.	
	11th		23 rounds expended in M.G's at X.23.c.80.90. 1 O.R. admitted to hospital sick.	
			11 guns in action.	
	12th		1 O.R. evacuated to C.C.S. (sprained ankle). 11 guns in action	
	13th		2 O.R. admitted to hospital. 11 guns in action.	
	14th		1 Officer and 9 O.R's to 1/2th Army T.M. Course. 7 Reinforcements obtained from 1st Army Reinforcement Camp.	
			11 guns in action	

Army Form C. 2118.

WAR DIARY
or
INTELLIGENCE SUMMARY.
(Erase heading not required.)

Instructions regarding War Diaries and Intelligence Summaries are contained in F. S. Regs., Part II. and the Staff Manual respectively. Title pages will be prepared in manuscript.

Place	Date	Hour	Summary of Events and Information	Remarks and references to Appendices
In the field	15th		27 rounds expended in Lubrication with Artillery Bombardment	
			Sgt. C. Swetenham left Unit for Base by base train. 1 gun in action	
	16th		12 guns bolt received from D.A.D.O.S.	
	17th		1 O.R. returned to duty from hospital. 11 guns in action	
			Cpl. Sherar promoted Rank of A/Sgt vice Sgt. L. Swetenham. 1 O.R. returned to duty from hospital. 11 guns in action	
	18th		5 rounds expended on Jerry house at X.14.b. 95.75. 11 guns in action	
	19th		15 rounds expended on X.14.b. 85.75. and 14 rounds expended on Jerry ob. X.24.d. 36.70. 1 gun in action	
	20th		Received 16 rounds T.M.G. & 2 T.M. set box ammunition from R.E's. 11 guns in action	
	21st		10 rifle grns camouflage ammunition trunk, balls camouflage rifles 140. T.M.G. components and 100 charges received from Held Ord. Bush Store. 11 guns in action	
	25th		1 gun out of action (replacements found). 1 O.R. admitted Khazine Subs. 10 guns in action	
	26th		2 O.R. joined from 4th Dist. Receptions Camp. 10 guns in action	
	27th		9 rounds expended on new trench at X.30.a.73.91 with gun mounts. 10 guns in action	
	28th		1 O.R. returned from Fd. Ambi. R.A. Rest Camp. 10 guns in action	

Army Form C. 2118.

WAR DIARY
or
INTELLIGENCE SUMMARY
(Erase heading not required.)

Instructions regarding War Diaries and Intelligence Summaries are contained in F. S. Regs., Part II. and the Staff Manual respectively. Title pages will be prepared in manuscript.

Place	Date	Hour	Summary of Events and Information	Remarks and references to Appendices
Little Hill	29.1		50 rounds expended on M.G. at X.23.a. 80.00 and X.23.c.85.91 with good effect	
			10 guns in action	
	30.1.		21 rounds expended on House at X.16.d.50.16. 7 direct hits and house destroyed	
			10 guns in action	

3.4.18

Aubrey Paulson Capt.
4/6/6 D.T.M.O.

WAR DIARY
INTELLIGENCE SUMMARY

461st Div. Trench Mortar Batteries

Army Form C. 2118

Vol 27

Place	Date	Hour	Summary of Events and Information	Remarks and references to Appendices
In the Field	1st.		X Battery fired 8 rounds at M.G. at X.14.b.57.90. M.G. silenced. 10 guns in action.	
	2nd.		1 O.R. returned to duty from hospital. 10 guns in action	
	3rd.		Y Battery fired 10 rounds on L.T.M. Emplacement (X.24.c.28.61.) 6 rolls camouflage received from 1st Corps Camouflage Officer, and 1 box of 20 charges received from 461st Div. Bomb Store.	
	4th		X Battery fired 27 rounds in co-operation with Stokes Mortars. 10 guns in action.	
	5th.		1 O.R. joined from 461st Div. Reception Camp.	
	6th.		1 O.R. joined from A/231 Brigade R.F.A. 10 guns in action.	
	7th.		10 guns in action.	
	8th.		Y Battery fired 20 rounds on M.G. Emplacement (X.23.c.57.97.) 10 guns in action	
	9th.		1 gun destroyed by shell-fire. 9 guns in action. Lieut. Butler granted leave to U.K.	
	10th.		Cpl. Rowsley transferred to England, for temporary Commission in R.F.A. 9 guns in action	
	11th.		X Battery fired 36 rounds on cellars. T.M.'s and M.G's. Y Battery fired 46 rounds on M.G. posts. 1 Officer and 9 O.R's returned from 5th Army Trench Mortar School	

Army Form C. 2118.

WAR DIARY
or
INTELLIGENCE SUMMARY.
(Erase heading not required.)

Place	Date	Hour	Summary of Events and Information	Remarks and references to Appendices
In the field	11th.		9 guns in action.	
	12th.		Y Battery fired 25 rounds on X.23.c.90.90. to X.16.d. 80.15. 2 O.Rs. to X.III Corps Rest Camp. 9 guns in action. 1 O.R. admitted to hospital. 1 Officer returned from leave to U.K. 1 O.R. returned from leave to U.K.	
	13th.		Y Battery fired 30 rounds on various targets. Several direct hits were obtained. 9 guns in action.	
	14th.		Received 300 rounds T.M.G. from H.6th. Div. Bomb Store. 2 guns to I.O.M. for repair. 10 guns in action.	
	15th.		10 guns in action.	
	16th.		Y Battery fired 35 rounds on New Enemy work and L.T.M's. with excellent results. 10 guns in action.	
	17th.		X Battery fired 10 rounds on fortified cellars. Y Battery fired 40 rounds on various targets, obtaining several direct hits. 10 guns in action.	
	18th.		Y Battery fired 20 rounds on enemy O.P. 4 direct hits were obtained. 10 guns in action. 1 O.R. admitted to hospital.	

Army Form C. 2118.

WAR DIARY
or
INTELLIGENCE SUMMARY.
(Erase heading not required.)

Instructions regarding War Diaries and Intelligence Summaries are contained in F. S. Regs., Part II. and the Staff Manual respectively. Title pages will be prepared in manuscript.

JULY 1918

Place	Date	Hour	Summary of Events and Information	Remarks and references to Appendices
In the field	19th		2 OR's to XIII Corps R.A. Rest Camp. Y Battery fired 45 rounds on various targets. Several direct hits being obtained. 10 guns in action.	
	20th		X Battery fired 20 rounds on M.G. and cellars. 10 guns in action.	
	21st		Received 250 rounds T.M.G. X Battery fired 6 rounds at House (X.8.C.58.46) 2Lieut L.G. Northfield granted leave to U.K. 10 guns in action.	
	22nd.		Received 150 rounds T.M.G. 1 OR. returned to duty from hospital. 10 guns in action	
	23rd.		Received 200 rounds T.M.G. 2 guns condemned by I.O.M. 13th O.M.W. (L) and returned to D.A.D.O.S. 10 guns in action.	
	24th		1 OR returned to duty from hospital.	
	25th		X Battery fired 20 rounds on cellar, and adjacent M.G. Y Battery fired 16 rounds OSE de RAUX, 3 direct hits being obtained. 1 officer returned from leave to U.K.	
	26th		2 OR's returned from XIII Corps R.A. Rest Camp, and 2 OR's to XIII Corps R.A. Rest Camp	
	28th		X Battery fired 10 rounds on X14.b.85.70. Y Battery fired 20 rounds on PILL Box at (X.7.C.20.70) 10 guns in action	

WAR DIARY or INTELLIGENCE SUMMARY

Army Form C. 2118.

JULY 1918

Place	Date	Hour	Summary of Events and Information	Remarks and references to Appendices
In the field	29th		10 guns in action	
	31st		X Battery fired 23 rounds on house and M.Gs. Retaliation, 50 rounds L.T.M.S. 10 guns in action	

Aubrey Paulin Capt.

46th. D.T.M.O.

3.8.18

CONFIDENTIAL

— WAR DIARY —

6th: DIVISIONAL TRENCH MORTAR BATTERIES.

AUGUST 1st: to 31st: 1918.

WAR DIARY
INTELLIGENCE SUMMARY.

AUGUST 1918

46th Divl. Trench Mortar Batteries

Army Form C. 2118.

Vol 30

Place	Date	Hour	Summary of Events and Information	Remarks and references to Appendices
In the Field	1st.		Cpl Snoston returned to duty from 5th Army Reinforcement Camp. 10 guns in action.	
	2nd.		2 OR's granted leave to U.K. X. Battery fired 14 rounds on House and M.G. X/5. G. 20.80 and 2 OR's to XIII Corps Rest Camp and 2 OR's returned from XIII Corps Rest Camp. X/14. G. 95.70.	
	3rd.		Y Battery fired 5 rounds on enemy strong points. 10 guns in action. a) X.22.G.46.95.	
	4th.		X Battery fired 15 rds on T.M. and snipers house. 10 guns in action. (X.8.2 20.60. & X.14.G.80.80)	
	5th.		1 OR slightly wounded. 1 OR admitted to hospital. X Battery fired 11 rounds on house and T.M. position. 9.G.18.05 guns X/14 30.80) Y.23.a 55.33, Y.23 a.60.50, Y.23.a. 60.68.	
	6th.		Y Battery fired 25 rds on M.G. post. a) 10 guns in action.	
	7th.		X Batt'y fired 42 rds on house and T.M. positions. Enemy working parties dispersed. (being X/3. Buttes R.F.A.) 1 officer and 1 OR to 1st Army School of Mortars. 2 OR's to 1st Army Rest Camp. X.2.d 10.60.+ X/14 G 90.70 + X/15.d 15.05	
	9th.		1 T.M. and 159 rds T.M.G. destroyed by hostile shell fire. 2 OR's returned to duty from 5th Army Reinforcement Camp. 11 guns in action.	
	9th.		2 OR's to XIII Corps Rest Camp and 2 OR's returned from XIII Corps Rest Camp. 1 OR admitted to hospital (2Lieut A. Gorloi D.M.H)	
	10th.		1 officer joined from 230th Brigade R.F.A. 11 guns in action.	

Army Form C. 2118.

WAR DIARY
or
INTELLIGENCE SUMMARY.
(Erase heading not required.)

AUGUST 1918.

Instructions regarding War Diaries and Intelligence Summaries are contained in F.S. Regs., Part II. and the Staff Manual respectively. Title pages will be prepared in manuscript.

Place	Date	Hour	Summary of Events and Information	Remarks and references to Appendices
In the field	11th		2 ORs to XIII Corps Gas School. 11 guns in action.	
	12th		Received 160 rds T.M.G. from 46th Div. Bomb Store. Y Battery fired 10 rds on M.G. at X.23.a.80.75	
	13th		1 gun and 2 gun belts received from D.A.D.O.S. 46th Div. Bomb. Stow. 11 guns in action. X Battery fired 10 rds on House and M.G. at X(16.d.95.15) Y Battery fired 15 rds on PILL BOX at X.7.d.3.13 with good effect, and 2 rds on M.G. nest. 1 gun destroyed by premature 2 ORs killed and 1 OR badly wounded. Received 130 T.M.G. component parts 10 guns in action.	
	14th		Lieut. J.W. Hewitt M.C. R.F.A. wounded in action. 4 ORs to 46th. D.A. Signals. 10 guns in action.	
	15th		11 guns in action.	X.16.b.10.90 and X.8.b.80.30
	16th		X Battery fired 30 rds in 2 ORs to XIII Corps Rest camp and 2 ORs returned from XIII Corps Rest camp. Gun Collins promoted to S/Sgt/Bdr from 13.8.18. 1 OR reported died of wounds 14.8.18.	
	17th		4 ORs granted leave to U.K. 11 guns in action (Shun. L.J. Gilkinson R.F.A.)	
	18th		1 OR returned from leave to U.K. 1 Officer joined from 231 Brigade R.F.A. Sgt. J.D. Kimble transferred to Base. 11 guns in action.	
	19th		1 OR granted 1 mnth (re-engagement) leave to U.K. 1 OR admitted Hospital Sick.	

Army Form C. 2118.

WAR DIARY
INTELLIGENCE SUMMARY
(Erase heading not required.)

AUGUST 1918.

Instructions regarding War Diaries and Intelligence Summaries are contained in F. S. Regs., Part II. and the Staff Manual respectively. Title pages will be prepared in manuscript.

Place	Date	Hour	Summary of Events and Information	Remarks and references to Appendices
In the field	20th		X Battery fired 5 rds on M.G. and obtained 3 direct hits. 11 guns in action.	
	21st		1 OR granted special leave to U.K. 2 OR's to 1st Army Rest Camp, and 1 OR returned from 1st Army Rest Camp. 1 gun received from D.A.O.O.S. 461th Div. 11 guns in action.	
	22nd		1 gun to 13th. T.O.M. for repairs. 4 OR's granted leave to U.K. 10 guns in action. 1 Officer and 1 OR returned from 1st Army School of Mortars.	
	23rd		10 guns in action	
	25th		2 OR's returned from XIII Corps Gas Course. Received 200 charges and 100 component parts from 461th Div. Bomb Store. 10 guns in action. (Capt L.A. Russell M.C.)	
	26th		D.T.M.O. granted leave to U.K. 10 guns in action. (A/Major L.F. McHutchon R.F.A.)	
	27th		1 Officer returned from leave to U.K. 10 guns in action.	
	28th		4 OR's granted leave to U.K. 1 gun returned from 13th. T.O.M. 10 guns in action.	
	29th		X Battery fired 16 rds from Mobile T.M. on various targets. 10 guns in action.	X.3.d.55.65. = 7.c.5.15.60. X.3.2.9.37.
	30th		2 OR's to XIII Corps Rest Camp and 2 OR's returned from XIII Corps Rest Camp.	
	31st		10 guns in action.	

for D.T.M.O.
4/6th D.A.

3.9.18.

SEPTEMBER 1918.

WAR DIARY
or
INTELLIGENCE SUMMARY
(Erase heading not required.)

Army Form C. 2118.

46th Div. T.M.B's.

Vol 31

Place	Date	Hour	Summary of Events and Information	Remarks and references to Appendices
In the field	1st		1OR to Signalling School. 10 guns in action.	
	2nd		1OR to School of Cookery. 10 guns in action.	
	3rd		Junct Mortar Batteries moved into rest billets at E.18.6. 40.30. 10 guns in action.	
	4th		4 OR's to 1st Army Rest Camp. 2 guns in action. 6 at moved dump. 3 prisoners MG's in Juv T	
	5th		All T.M. guns, stores and ammunition (exc'd 1 of T.M. H.Q. 5 reinforcements (exc'd from 46th. D.A.C) withdrawn from line. Guns and stores dumped at T.M. H.Q. Ammunition dump established at E.15.6. 28.33.	
	6th		T.M. Batteries moved to CHARTREUSE CHATEAU, GOSNAY.	
	7th		3 OR's returned from leave to U.K.	
	8th		1 OR granted leave to U.K. 1 OR returned from leave to U.K. 1 sub. returned to 896E 1 gun to 13th I.O.M. O.M.W. 11 guns in possession.	
	9th		1 OR granted leave to U.K. 2 sub. h.o.s, 2 wells camouflage returned to N.M. Dump	
	10th		1 OR granted leave to U.K.	
	11th		2 OR's returned from XIII Corps Rest Camp. 1 OR granted leave to U.K. 1 gun returned from 13th I.C.M. O.M.W.	
	12th		T.M.B's moved to Railhead, LILLERS. 1 OR returned from leave to U.K.	

WAR DIARY
or
INTELLIGENCE SUMMARY.
(Erase heading not required.)

Army Form C. 2118.

SEPTEMBER. 1918.   46th. Divl. T.M. B/s

Place	Date	Hour	Summary of Events and Information	Remarks and references to Appendices
In the field	12th.		2 OR's granted leave to U.K.	
	13th.		"Y" Battery entrained at LILLERS. T.M.B's detrained at HEILLY. Corpl. C. A. Pantolow M.C. (D.T.M.O.)	
			returned from leave to U.K. 1 OR granted leave to U.K. T.M.B's moved into billets at	
			BONNAY.	
	14th.		Corpl. C. Porter R.F.A. granted leave to U.K. 2 OR's returned from leave to U.K.	
	15th.			
	16th.			
	17th.		2 OR's returned from leave to U.K.	
	18th.			
	19th.		46th Divl. T.M. B's moved from BONNAY and took over billets at MONS-EN-CHAUSSEE.	
	20th.			
	21st.		4 OR's returned from 1st Army Rest Camp. 1 OR returned from Cookery Course	
	22nd.		1 OR returned from leave to U.K. 1 OR granted leave to U.K. from 23-9-18 to 7-10-18.	
	23rd.			
	24th.		1 OR granted leave to U.K. from 25-9-18 to 9-10-18. General training, Gun Drill, map Reading. Laying etc	
			Camp Fatigues. # N.C.O's & 30 O.R's detailed for duty at 2 forward Dumps at Z.32.B.5.8 + R.16.B.5.5	

W. Bonhill. 2/Lt.
for D.T.M.O.
46th Divn. Arty.

WAR DIARY
or
INTELLIGENCE SUMMARY.
(Erase heading not required.)

Army Form C. 2118.

September 1918
#6H Dwl. T.M.B's

Place	Date	Hour	Summary of Events and Information	Remarks and references to Appendices
In the Field	24th		L.T.M.O and 2 Officers of X/46 Reconnoitred for positions; O.R. Y/46 and 2 hers ditto.	
	26th		1 Officer, 3 N.C.O's and 21 O.Rs detailed to Build positions in line G.27.C.90.40 1 Gun. G.27.C.98.90 1 Gun. G.27.C.90.20. 1 Gun. G.24.C.95.15. 1 Gun. Detail still at A.R.P.	
	26th		2 O.Rs Granted leave to U.K from 21/9/18 to 11/10/18. Two O.Rs returned from leave to U.K. 1 Officer, 8 N.C.O's and 8 O.Rs from each Battery went forward to Build Gun Positions. Remainder with the exception of detail at A.R.P. on Camp Fatigues, Cpl Key wounded.	
No.820634 / 27th Cpl Key, died of wounds	27/10/18		The Brigade moved forward to Bullils at R.8.A.45. Go Carrying 2 Guards each of 1 hco and 3 men.	
	28th		1 Officer and 2 detachments of Each Battery at Gun Positions getting guns in, and ammunition up. 1 Officer and 2 detachments of X and Y/46 firing on selected targets. # Guns in Action. Remainder at new Billets digging in etc.	
	29th		1. O.R. Granted leave to U.K from 29/9/18 to 13/10/18. detachments returned from the line carrying Guard with Guns. of 1 N.C.O and 3 men	
	30th		2 O.Rs. Granted leave to U.K. from 1/10/18 to 15/10/18. 2 O.Rs returned from leave to U.K.	

R. Morville 2/L. RFA
for L.T.M.O
46" Dw. Art"

CONFIDENTIAL.

WAR DIARY.

TRENCH MORTAR BATTERIES.

OCTOBER 1st: to OCTOBER 31st: 1918.

WAR DIARY
INTELLIGENCE SUMMARY
(Erase heading not required.)

Army Form C. 2118.

46th. Divl. T.M.B's.

OCTOBER 1918.

Place	Date	Hour	Summary of Events and Information	Remarks and references to Appendices
In the field	1st.		3 OR's granted leave to U.K. 3 OR's returned from leave to U.K. Corpl. L. Potts. R.F.A. returned from leave to U.K.	
	2nd.		3 OR's granted leave to U.K. Capt. R.J. Thornton M.C. and Lieut D.J. Strachan R.F.A. granted leave to U.K. (3as)	
	3rd.		3 OR's granted leave to U.K.	
	4th.		Salved in line, 3 Light (3") Minenwerfers T.M.B's complete, (minus 2 elinos) 3 OR's granted leave to U.K.	
	5th.		3. N.C.O.'s and 27 men attached for duty to A.R.P. Experimental shoot with light (3") minenwerfers.	
	6th.		Experimental shooting with light (3") Minenwerfers, and training in camp area.	
	8th.		10 OR's attached for duty at A.R.P.	
	10th.		1 OR returned from leave to U.K.	
	11th.		46th. Divl. T.M.B's moved into billets at FRESNOY-LE-GRAND. (I.8.c.20.65)	
	12th.		1 OR returned from leave to U.K.	
	13th.		1 OR returned from leave to U.K.	

WAR DIARY
INTELLIGENCE SUMMARY
(Erase heading not required.)

Army Form C. 2118.

46th. DNL. T.M.B's

OCTOBER 1918.

Instructions regarding War Diaries and Intelligence Summaries are contained in F. S. Regs., Part II. and the Staff Manual respectively. Title pages will be prepared in manuscript.

Place	Date	Hour	Summary of Events and Information	Remarks and references to Appendices
In the field	14th		2 OR's granted leave to U.K. Lieut. J.J. Loutchert, R.F.A. rejoined 231. Bde R.F.A.	
	15th		2 OR's granted leave to U.K.	
	16th		Lieut. F.H. Hole, R.F.A. attached to 230th. Bde R.F.A. 2 OR's granted leave to U.K.	
	17th		X 46. and Y 46. T.M.B's fired 16H rounds from light (3") minenwerfer T.M.'s in co-operation with Artillery Bombardment. Targets:- E.13.d.52.40. - E.13.d.52.70 - E.13.d.60.85 - E.13.d.62.50. 2 OR's granted leave to U.K.	
	18th		2/Lieut. C.B. Northfield, R.F.A. attached for duty to H.Q.R.A. 2 OR's granted leave to U.K. 2 OR's returned from leave to U.K.	
	19th		2/Lieut. D.J. Strachan, R.F.A. returned from leave to U.K. 2 OR's granted leave to U.K.	
	20th		Cpl. R. Walker (X 46. T.M.B.) wounded at duty. 2. OR's granted leave to U.K. Capt. R.L. Hunter M.C. returned from leave to U.K. 1. OR. returned from leave to U.K.	
	21st		1. OR. admitted to hospital sick. 3. OR's returned from leave to U.K. 2 OR's granted leave to U.K.	
	22nd		Cpl. H. Scott. posted to 23rd. Bde. R.F.A. 3. OR's returned from leave to U.K. 2 OR's granted leave to U.K.	

OCTOBER 1918. 46th. DIV. T.M.B.

WAR DIARY
INTELLIGENCE SUMMARY.
(Erase heading not required.)

Army Form C. 2118.

Place	Date	Hour	Summary of Events and Information	Remarks and references to Appendices
In the field	23rd.		2 ORs granted leave to U.K.	
	24th		2 ORs granted leave to U.K.	
	25th.		1 OR. returned from leave to U.K. 2 ORs granted leave to U.K.	
	26th.		Lieut. H.J.K. Butler, R.F.A. admitted to hospital (sick) 3 ORs granted leave to U.K.	
	28th.		Lieut. A. Goldie, R.F.A. granted leave to U.K. 2. 6" T.M. beds, complete with Mobile carriage, received from No 1. O.M.W. (medium)	
	29th.		Capt. E. Coxter R.F.A. and Lieut D.J. Strachan R.F.A. admitted to hospital (sick)	
	31st.		Capt. C.A. Pantalen M.C. (D.T.M.O.) accidentally injured, and admitted to hospital.	

3.11.18

A. M. Waters Capt.
A/46th. D.T.M.O.

WAR DIARY

46th Divl. T.M. Batteries

INTELLIGENCE SUMMARY

November 1918

Place	Date	Hour	Summary of Events and Information	Remarks and references to Appendices
In the field	1st.		46th. Divl. T.M.B's moved into fresh billets at BOHAIN-LE-GRAND. (D.21.d.15.7.0.)	
	2nd.		Lieut. J.W.L. Merritt, M.C. R.F.A. rejoined X46 T.M.B. from Base.	
	3rd.		Capt. C.A. Pawlden M.C. (D.T.M.O.) returned from Hospital.	
	4th.		2 OR's returned from leave to U.K. 46th. Divl. T.M.B's moved into fresh billets at MOLAIN.	
	5th.		3 OR's returned from leave to U.K.	
	6th.			
	7th.		46th. Divl. T.M.B's moved into fresh billets at MEZIERES. 2 OR's returned from leave to U.K.	
	8th.		2 S OR's returned to Unit from A.B.P.	
	9th.		Lieut. C.C. Northfield R.F.A. posted to 230th. Bde. R.F.A. 1 OR. returned to duty from HQ. R.A.	
	10th.		3 OR's returned from leave to U.K.	
	11th.		6 OR's returned from leave to U.K.	
	12th.		2 OR's returned from leave to U.K.	
	13th.		Capt. C. Gorb, R.F.A. returned to X46 T.M.B. from Hospital. 1 OR. returned from leave to U.K.	
	14th.			
	15th.		Lieut. A. Goldie R.F.A. returned from leave to U.K. 3 OR's returned from leave to U.K.	

WAR DIARY

NOVEMBER 1918. 46th Divl. T.M. Batteries

INTELLIGENCE SUMMARY.

(Erase heading not required.)

Army Form C. 2118.

Instructions regarding War Diaries and Intelligence Summaries are contained in F. S. Regs., Part II, and the Staff Manual respectively. Title pages will be prepared in manuscript.

Place	Date	Hour	Summary of Events and Information	Remarks and references to Appendices
In the field	16th.		46th. Divl. T.M.Bs. moved into fresh billets at LANDRECIES. (G.23.a.05.90.)	
			1 O.R. returned from leave to U.K.	
	19th.		3. O.R.s returned from leave to U.K. 1 L.G.S. Wagon with team, and 1 O.R. attached to D.T.M.O.	
			2 mobile T.M. beds with carriages received from No. 2. O.M.W.	
	20th.		Gnr Dalby returned to 746th. T.M.B. from No. 7 Military Prison.	
	26th.		2 O.R.s returned to duty from Hospital in U.K.	
	27th.		1 O.R. admitted to hospital (Sick)	
	28th.			
	29th.			
	30th.		1 O.R. reports accidentally injured whilst salving ammunition.	

3rd. December 1918.

[signature] Captain.
46th. D.T.M.O.

WAR DIARY 46th. Divl. T.M.Bs.
or
INTELLIGENCE SUMMARY.
(Erase heading not required.)

Army Form C. 2118.

DECEMBER 1918.

Vol 34

Place	Date	Hour	Summary of Events and Information	Remarks and references to Appendices
In the field	1st		1 OR granted leave to U.K.	
	2nd		1 OR returned to duty from hospital	
	3rd		1 OR granted leave to U.K.	
	4th		1 OR admitted to hospital. 1 OR to 466 M.T. Coy. on Gasoline Course.	
	5th		NIL	
	6th			
	7th		Two OR Americans and 1 OR granted leave to U.K.	
	8th		NIL	
	9th			
	10th		Two book movers despatched to Internment Centre CAMBRAI	
	11th		1 OR granted leave to U.K.	
	12th		1 OR to Bricklaying Course. over 1 OR to Wireless Course at 466 Divl. Signal Coy.	
	13th		2 ORs on Lewis G.W.L. Course with M.G. R.F.A. attached to 137 Inf. Brigade for	
	14th		1 OR was despatched to Internment Centre CAMBRAI (salvage)	
	15th			
	16th		2 ORs to Course of Motor Drivers at 466. Divl. H.Q.	

WAR DIARY

INTELLIGENCE SUMMARY

DECEMBER 1918.   46th. Div. T.M.B's

Army Form C. 2118.

Place	Date	Hour	Summary of Events and Information	Remarks and references to Appendices
In the field	17th		10R granted leave to U.K.	
	18th		10R and 10R returned from leave to U.K.	
	19th		10R granted leave to U.K. 2 Cook Private despatched to Interpreting Centre CAMBRAI	
	20th		10R returned from leave to U.K.	
	21st		10R granted leave to U.K.	
	22nd			
	23rd		Lieut. W. L. Hewitt M.C. R.F.A. and 20 O.R. returned from 137 Brigade (Salvage Party)	
	24th		10R granted two wireless course and 10R returned from Painting course.	
	25th		10R granted leave to U.K.	
	26th			
	27th		NIL.	
	28th			
	29th		Lieut. Yard. Hewitt M.C. and 10R to GROSSLIERS G.H.Q. School of R.A. Gunnery.	
	30th		10R to No. 1 O.M.N. BOHAIN to Blacksmith course.	
	31st		10R granted Continental leave to BRUSSELS	

DECEMBER 1918. 46th Div. T.M.B's

Army Form C. 2118.

WAR DIARY
~~INTELLIGENCE~~ SUMMARY.
(Erase heading not required.)

Instructions regarding War Diaries and Intelligence Summaries are contained in F. S. Regs., Part II. and the Staff Manual respectively. Title pages will be prepared in manuscript.

Place	Date	Hour	Summary of Events and Information	Remarks and references to Appendices
In the Field	26.		108 returned from leave to U.K.	
			2Lieut A. Goldie and 21 OR's attached to 137th Inf. Brigade at FRESNOY-LE-GRAND.	
			2Lt D.J. Sheelan R.F.A rejoined Unit from Base.	
			A.J.Paul Lt	
			A/C O.C. 46th D.T.M.B.	
			3.1.19	

WAR DIARY
or
INTELLIGENCE SUMMARY

Army Form C. 2118.

46th Divl Ym. Bty. commencing Jan 1st 1919.

Wl. 35

Place	Date	Hour	Summary of Events and Information	Remarks and references to Appendices
LANDRECIES	1st		1 O.R. rejoined unit from 231 Bde R.F.A. 1 O.R. granted leave to Brussels.	
"	2nd		Gunners Gentry and Allison promoted to Rank of Bombardier.	
"	3rd		2/Lt. D. Strachan att. Y/46 T.M.B. 2 O.Rs despatched for demobilisation.	
"	4th		Gunner Martin awarded 28 days No.1 F.P.	
"	5th		1 O.R. rejoined from leave.	
"	6th		1 O.R. granted leave to U.K.	
"	7th			
"	8th		1 O.R. rejoined from course of Education.	
"	9th		1 O.R rejoining from leave	
"	10th		1 O.R. returned from leave to Brussels.	
"	11th		1 O.R. granted leave to U.K. 1 O.R. to course of Farming.	
"	12th		Gnr Grimes to Watford Details.	
"	13th		1 O.R. despatched for demob. 1 O.R admitted Hospital	
"	14th		4 O.Rs att. 139 Bde for Salvage. 1 O.R. to course of Wireless. Gnr. Martin. att 1st Monmouths to complete 28 days F.P. No.1.	
"	14th		Cpl. Dealey transferred to England.	
"	15th		1 O.R. granted leave to U.K.	
"	16th			
"	17th		6 O.R's to Area Bomnob. 1 O.R despatched for demob.	
"	18th		Bdr Lockwood promoted to Cpl. Bdr Hand promoted to Cpl. Gnr Smith. P. promoted to Bombardier. Gnr. Flick promoted to Bdr.	

Army Form C. 2118.

WAR DIARY
or
INTELLIGENCE SUMMARY.

46th Div. 2.M. Bty's commencing Jan. 18th 1919

(Erase heading not required.)

Instructions regarding War Diaries and Intelligence Summaries are contained in F. S. Regs., Part II. and the Staff Manual respectively. Title pages will be prepared in manuscript.

Place	Date	Hour	Summary of Events and Information	Remarks and references to Appendices
LANDRECIES	18th		2 O.R's despatched for demob.	
"	19th		1. O.R. admitted to Hospital. 1. O.R. att. to 139 3y Bde for Salvage.	
"	20th		3. O.R's despatched for demob.	
"	21st		1. O.R. granted leave to U.R. 1. O.R. despatched for demob.	
"	22nd		1. O.R. rejoined from Hospital. 2/Lt. Goldie rejoined from Fresnoy	
"			1. O.R's rejoined from Salvage Fresnoy. 1 O.R rejoined from 139 3y Bde.	
"	22nd		Lt. Alexander demobilised whilst on leave Aut. W6/25541 P.T.P.	
"	23rd		Bdr. Whitehouse promoted Cpl. 1 O.R. despatched for demob.	
"	24th		3. O.R's despatched for demob.	
"	25th		O.R's att Salvage Office Le Cateau. Capt Hunter proceeded to U.R. for demob.	
"	26th		For Ludforth to O.R.A. 1. O.R. despatched for demob. 1 O.R. leave to U.R.	
"	27th		Capt Paulden M.C. proceeded on leave to U.R. D.T.M. O's offices transferred	
"	28th		to Officers Mess. 1. O.R despatched for demob.	
"	29th		Lt Hewitt rejoined from A.A. Gunnery School.	
"	30		2 O.R's to Area Commdt La Groise.	

Army Form C. 2118.

WAR DIARY 46 Div. T.M. Btys.

or

INTELLIGENCE SUMMARY. commencing 30 Jan 1919.

(Erase heading not required.)

Instructions regarding War Diaries and Intelligence Summaries are contained in F. S. Regs., Part II. and the Staff Manual respectively. Title pages will be prepared in manuscript.

Place	Date	Hour	Summary of Events and Information	Remarks and references to Appendices
LANDRECIES	30		Bor Fisher promoted to bot. Gnr Hall promoted to Bombardier.	
February	1st			
	2nd		Capt E. Ports despatched to Winchester for Repatriation.	
	3rd		French Motor Batteries affiliated to D.A.C.	

M. Naubte. Capt.
46th D.T.M.O.

www.ingramcontent.com/pod-product-compliance
Lightning Source LLC
Chambersburg PA
CBHW082011220426
43670CB00014B/2602